The Twitter Book

by Tim O'Reilly and Sarah Milstein

O'REILLY®

Beijing · Cambridge · Farnham · Köln · Sebastopol · Taipei · Tokyo

The Twitter Book
by Tim O'Reilly and Sarah Milstein

Copyright © 2009 Tim O'Reilly and Sarah Milstein
Printed in Canada.

Published by O'Reilly Media, Inc., 1005 Gravenstein Highway North, Sebastopol, CA 95472.

O'Reilly books may be purchased for educational, business, or sales promotional use. Online editions are also available for most titles (http://my.safaribooksonline.com). For more information, contact our corporate/institutional sales department: (800) 998-9938 or corporate@oreilly.com.

Editor: Joe Wikert

Production Editor: Adam Witwer

Proofreader: Marlowe Shaeffer

Indexer: Sarah Milstein

Design: Monica Kamsvaag, Suzy Wivott, Ron Bilodeau, and Edie Freedman

Printing History:
First Edition: June, 2009

ISBN: 9780596802813

[CK]   [06/09]

ABOUT THE AUTHORS

Tim O'Reilly (@timoreilly)

Tim O'Reilly is the founder and CEO of O'Reilly Media, Inc., thought by many to be the best computer book publisher in the world. O'Reilly Media also hosts conferences on technology topics, including the Web 2.0 Summit, the Web 2.0 Expo, the O'Reilly Open Source Convention, and the O'Reilly Emerging Technology Conference. Tim's blog, the O'Reilly Radar, "watches the alpha geeks" to determine emerging technology trends, and serves as a platform for advocacy about issues of importance to the technical community. Tim is an activist for open source and open standards, and an opponent of software patents and other incursions of new intellectual property laws into the public domain. Tim's long-term vision for his company is to change the world by spreading the knowledge of innovators. For everything Tim, see *tim.oreilly.com*.

Sarah Milstein (@SarahM)

Sarah Milstein frequently writes, speaks and teaches on Twitter. She is also cofounder of 20slides. com, a site for lively, work-related workshops. Previously, she was on the senior editorial staff at O'Reilly, where she founded the Tools of Change for Publishing conference (TOC) and led the development of the Missing Manuals, a best-selling series of computer books for non-geeks. She's written for the series, too, coauthoring *Google: The Missing Manual*. Before joining O'Reilly, Sarah was a freelance writer and editor, and a regular contributor to *The New York Times*. She was also a program founder for Just Food, a local-food-and-farms non-profit, and cofounder of Two Tomatoes Records, a label that distributes and promotes the work of children's musician Laurie Berkner.

CONTENTS

v

#TwitterBook

The hashtag for this book is #TwitterBook

Hashtag? Whaaat?

A hashtag is a term, prefixed by the # symbol, that helps people categorize messages in Twitter. In Chapters 1 and 3, we explain how they work and how you can use them in a bunch of cool ways.

If you're already comfortable with hashtags, we encourage you to use this one if you want to twitter about our book. We'll be excited to see messages about how the book has helped you, but we truly welcome posts that point out things we can improve or add. If we use your tip in a future edition, we'll credit you, so don't hold back!

Introduction

In March 2006, a little communications service called Twttr debuted. It began as a side project at a San Francisco podcasting company, but it wasn't long before the side project became the main event.

Today, just three years later, Twitter is booming. The service has more than 10 million avid users, its web traffic was up nearly 131 percent from February to March 2009,* and unique visitors grew 1382 percent from February 2008 to February 2009.† You read that right: *1382 percent.*

This book will help you understand what happened in between—the ways Twitter is useful and addictive and unlike any other communications service—and how you can tap that power.

* Comscore, April 2009 (http://www.comscore.com/blog/2009/04/breaking_news_and_making_news.html); web traffic is only part of the picture for Twitter, because they get a significant amount of traffic from their API and some from SMS

† Nielsen NetView, February 2009 (http://blog.nielsen.com/nielsenwire/online_mobile/twitters-tweet-smell-of-success)

twitter

To all twitterers , if u c me n public come say hi, we r not the same we r from twitteronia, we connect

3:37 PM Feb 19th from txt

 THE_REAL_SHAQ

What is Twitter?

Twitter is a messaging service that shares a lot of characteristics with communication tools you already use. It has elements that are similar to email, IM, texting, blogging, RSS, social networks and so forth. But a few factors, particularly in combination, make Twitter unique:

Messages you send and receive on Twitter are no more than 140 characters, or about the length of a news headline. That means they're **really easy to write and read.**

Messages on Twitter are public, like blog posts, and you don't have to give people permission to see what you've written. That means **you can readily meet new people on Twitter.**

The messages are opt-in, and people choose to get a stream of others' messages. (On Twitter, this model is called "following.") That means **you have to be interesting,** or people will choose not to get your updates.

You can send and receive the messages via a variety of mechanisms, including mobile phones, PCs, websites and desktop programs, and they're distributed in real time. That means that Twitter can **fit with nearly anyone's workflow.**

When you add all that together, and you throw in a dose of the friendliness common on Twitter today, you get a powerful and appealing communications platform that turns out to be highly useful for a slew of personal and professional needs.

What's Twitter good for?
Ambient intimacy

Twitter poses the question, "What are you doing?" Sometimes, people answer pretty dutifully. So they're eating bacon for lunch, catching up on email run amok or cleaning the tub. Because they can send updates not only from their computers but from their mobile phones, too, people also report that they're ordering a triple double at In-N-Out Burger, sitting in traffic on Route 1 or boarding a plane for Omaha.

Although status updates like that may sound mundane, people on Twitter have found that becoming aware of what your friends, family and colleagues are doing (without having to respond) leads to a **lightweight but meaningful connection,** sometimes called "ambient awareness" or "ambient intimacy," a term coined by Leisa Reichelt (@leisa).

Tim on ambient intimacy: I see my brother James every couple of months, talk to him about as often, always wish for more. Through Twitter, I follow him every day. Of course, we have shared context that others may miss. Naturally, he tears up at a space launch: when we were kids we used to pray each night for a UFO to come down in our backyard. And it's great to know that he's got an exterminator in to deal with the biting spiders that kept me from staying over last time I visited. I know, as few do, that his background is a photo from my father's grave in Ireland.

Sarah on ambient intimacy: My brother and his wife had a baby recently, and part of the joy for me is seeing my parents become utterly smitten grandparents. Little messages about their experiences make me feel a lot closer than the 3,000 miles that separate us. (The DDOJ is the Daily Dose of Jack—photos of my nephew that family sends every day.)

What's Twitter good for?
Sharing news and commentary

But ambient intimacy isn't the only thing Twitter turns out to be good for. As the service has gained users, people are using it more and more to talk about what they're reading, watching, listening to and thinking about—often with links to the good stuff. Twitter has thus become a key player in the attention economy, **distributing ideas and comments about what people care about and what they have expertise in.**

twitter Think Big... The Rest Will Follow

Home Profile Find People Settings Help Sign out

http://twitpic.com/135xa - There's a plane in the Hudson. I'm on the ferry going to pick up the people. Crazy.

12:36 PM Jan 15th from TwitPic

jkrums
Jānis Krums

twitter

Home Profile Find People Settings Help Sign out

Our immediate response to the earthquake? Get in a doorway? Get under the desk? Nope. "Check Twitter!"

10:42 AM Mar 30th from web

veen
Jeffrey Veen

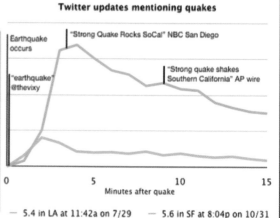

Twitter updates mentioning quakes

Earthquake occurs

"Strong Quake Rocks SoCal" NBC San Diego

"earthquake" @thevixy

"Strong quake shakes Southern California" AP wire

0   5   10   15

Minutes after quake

— 5.4 in LA at 11:42a on 7/29   — 5.6 in SF at 8:04p on 10/31

What's Twitter good for?
Breaking news and shared experiences

Twitter is the world's real-time newspaper. In January 2009, within minutes of the US Airways plane landing in the Hudson River, a nearby ferry passenger had twittered a picture and comment—scooping the professional news media on a story happening in their own backyard.

Twitter has also turned out to be one of the world's best seismograph, as people twitter en masse about earthquakes the instant they happen. The blue line on the chart shows twittering about the July 2008 earthquake in Los Angeles, along with the first mainstream media announcement. What Obi-Wan Kenobi said first in *Star Wars*—"I felt a great disturbance in the Force, as if millions of voices suddenly cried out"—Twitter has now made true.

The service has thus become **a great tool for sharing common experiences.** Those include not only emergencies, like natural disasters and terrorist attacks, but also organized events, like conferences and concerts. While a surge of messages on Twitter can break news, the individual posts help people verify what's happening, connect with resources, and, during emergencies, let others know whether they're safe.

What's Twitter good for? Mind reading

Whether you have an account on Twitter or not, the site's search service is **an amazing mind-reading tool, letting you see not just what individuals are thinking about, but what groups are focusing on, too.**

A well-honed search can reveal how other people feel about your company, your latest public talk and your favorite TV show. The ten trending topics that appear on the search page and change constantly give you insight into the things a lot of people find important at any given moment.

Key to this element of Twitter is that the search results update in *real time*. Here you can see two recent Tuesday morning searches. We took the top screenshot as Obama was wrapping up a speech; the 191 new results showed up within less than a minute. In the bottom screenshot, the fresh results took about ten minutes to accumulate.

What's Twitter good for?
Business conversations

Finally, Twitter is emerging as **a key business channel,** letting companies engage with customers, partners and other constituents in a direct way that's both personal and public—something no other medium allows.

Businesses are monitoring what people think of their products, responding to customer service requests, having conversations with stakeholders and making money through creative promotions of various kinds.

Celebrities, themselves mini-businesses, are engaging with their fans in new ways. Consider Shaquille O'Neal's "Random Acts of Shaqness," in which he uses Twitter to connect with fans in person before games. (On second thought, at 7'1" and more than 1,000,000 Twitter followers, we're not sure you can refer to Shaq as a "mini" anything.)

That covers just a few of the biggest uses of Twitter. So far. In the last few months, Twitter's growth has become exponential. That's not just the number of users, but also clever new uses for the platform and amazing third-party tools. You'll come up with new uses yourself.

CHAPTER 1 | Get Started

Twitter lives a dual life. On the one hand, it's a simple service. Besides letting you share and read very short messages, it has few bells and whistles. On the other hand, it can be surprisingly hard to figure out. The screens aren't particularly intuitive, and the jargon and symbols are obscure. Even more vexing, it's not clear at first why people are so enthusiastic about Twitter. **What makes it fun? Useful? Revolutionary?**

In the Introduction, we showed you a few great uses for Twitter. In this chapter, we help you get set up and explain some key ways to communicate successfully on the service. We also decode the most common jargon and symbols. (By the way, if you need a version of Twitter that works with assistive technologies, try **Accessible Twitter** [http://accessibletwitter.com]).

Of course, listening to others is one of the things Twitter is best for—and you don't need an account to do it. If you're all about tuning into the buzz, skip ahead to Chapter 2.

Join the Conversation

Already use Twitter on your phone? Finish signup now.

Already on Twitter? Sign in.

Full name   **Amanda Jones**   ✔ ok

Username   **AmaJos**   ✔ ok

Your URL: http://twitter.com/**AmaJos**

Password   ●●●●●●●   ✔ Good

Email   **Amanda.Jones@email.cc**   ✔ ok

☐ I want the inside scoop—please send me email updates!

bland **reproof**

Can't read this?
↻ Get two new words
🔊 Listen to the words

Powered by reCAPTCHA.
Help

Type the words above

Create my account

20

Sign up

Signing up takes just a few minutes. Head to **Twitter** (http://twitter.com) and click the Get Started button.

The first screen you see looks like the one here. The key pieces here are the name boxes. In the Full Name box, type your actual name (or your company name, if this is a corporate account). The Username box is where you add your account name—the one everybody on Twitter will know you by (like The_Real_Shaq or Pistachio or timoreilly). **For the username, try to find one with the fewest number of characters possible;** that becomes important as soon as people want to refer to you or repost your comments and find that your username is taking up several of their 140 characters.

After you fill out the rest and click "Create my account," Twitter walks you through another few steps to find your friends on the service and suggest people you might want to follow. Following is described later in this chapter.

Turn the page for quick tips on fleshing out your account so that other people find it appealing.

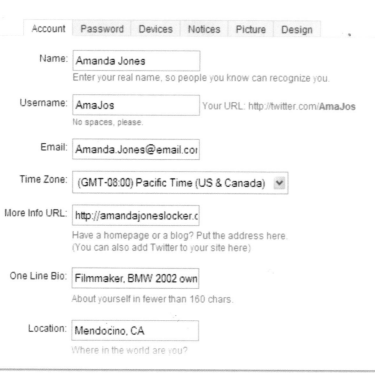

twitter

Home Profile Find People Settings Help Sign out

o_O Amanda Jones

| Account | Password | Devices | Notices | Picture | Design |

Name: `Amanda Jones`

Enter your real name, so people you know can recognize you.

Username: `AmaJos` Your URL: http://twitter.com/**AmaJos**

No spaces, please.

Email: `Amanda.Jones@email.cor`

Time Zone: `(GMT-08:00) Pacific Time (US & Canada)` ⌄

More Info URL: `http://amandajoneslocker.c`

Have a homepage or a blog? Put the address here.
(You can also add Twitter to your site here)

One Line Bio: `Filmmaker, BMW 2002 own`

About yourself in fewer than 160 chars.

Location: `Mendocino, CA`

Where in the world are you?

Account

From here you can change your basic account info, fill in your profile data, and set whether you want to be private or public.

Tips

- Filling in your profile information will help people find you on Twitter. For example, you'll be more likely to turn up in a Twitter search if you've added your location or your real name.

- Change your Twitter user name anytime without affecting your existing updates, @replies, direct messages, or other data. After changing it, make sure to let your followers know so you'll continue receiving all of your messages with your new user name.

- Protect your profile to keep your Twitter updates private. Approve who can follow you and keep your updates out

Quickly create a compelling profile

As soon as you create an account on Twitter, people can—and often will—start checking out your page, particularly if you follow them first. So **before you start clicking around, spend three minutes setting up your profile.** To get to the account page, head to the upper-right corner of your Twitter home page, and then click Settings (on some accounts, the link is below your account name).

When you get to the screen that looks like this, adjust the time zone, and then type in a URL that helps people learn more about you. It can be your blog, website, LinkedIn profile, etcetera.

Now comes the fun part: the Bio box, which gives you just 160 characters to tell your life story. Some people do it with a series of words or phrases, like David Pogue: "Tech columnist, NY Times; CNBC tech dude; Missing Manuals creator, dad of 3!" Some people tell a little story, like Miriam Salpeter: "As a career coach and resume writer, I encourage, enlighten and empower job seekers by offering job hunting and networking tips, interviewing advice and more."

Next, fill out your location (if you don't, you'll show up in fewer search results). Finally, if you want to keep your messages private, click "Protect my updates." (Most people leave them public.) When you're done, click Save.

One last step: head to the Picture tab and upload a photo, drawing or logo. Nothing says, "I'm a newbie and maybe a spammer" like the default icon.

Understand what "following" means

With the exception of accounts that have been protected, messages on Twitter are public. Like blog posts, anyone can see them. But the way nearly everyone sees other people's messages is by choosing to get a stream of the updates from people they're interested in. On Twitter, the opt-in model is called *following*. Here you can see that more than 2,000 people have chosen to follow Kat Meyer.

When you follow somebody, you receive a message every time he updates. When somebody follows you, he receives your message every time you update. Unlike a lot of social software, however, following on Twitter is what geeks call *asymmetric*. That is, **you don't have to agree to follow each other in order to see somebody's messages.**

There are two key implications of this model:

1. Because you don't have to verify each other, you're much more likely on Twitter than other social networks to find people you don't already know. That makes the site good for professional networking.

2. If you aren't interesting, people will unfollow you, or they'll never follow you in the first place. The opt-in arrangement means that Twitter rewards interestingness. Use your 140 characters wisely.

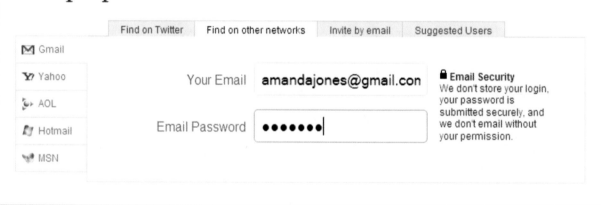

Find the people you know on Twitter

Twitter gives you a couple of tools to **discover people you already know who are twittering.** At the top of your Twitter account page, click Find People to get the tabs shown here. The two most useful tabs are:

"Find on Twitter," which lets you do a name search.

"Find on other networks," which checks your address book from Gmail, Yahoo, etcetera against all existing Twitter accounts. This option is especially handy, because a lot of people sign up for Twitter using their regular email address but a variation of their name you might not think to search for.

twitter tip

When you follow somebody on Twitter, he gets an email notification. Not to encourage stalking, but if you follow a person via RSS, he'll never know you're following him—or if you've unfollowed him. Grab the RSS feed for any Twitterer on his account page, right side, under the pics of people he's following.

twitter

What are you doing?

140

update

 anamariecox Making my day: Just saw a big buff guy in camo and captain's bars, walking a chihuahua.
9 minutes ago from Tweetie

 mashable 12omercials: 12 Second Video for Brands - http://bit.ly/150ZeD
20 minutes ago from web

 threadless It's a great day for hourly giveaways!!! Starting in 60 minutes on our Facebook fan page! Come watch.
http://www.facebook.com/thr...
22 minutes ago from CoTweet

 RyanSeacrest TMZ is reporting the celebrity killed in a car accident is Angels pitcher Nick Adenhart >http://twurl.nl/sl0664 - Sadao, Team Seacrest
23 minutes ago from TweetDeck

 anamariecox Joe and Mika are on 630AM from 10-12. PANTS STATUS: damp.
27 minutes ago from Tweetie

Get suggestions for cool people to follow

Twitter doesn't make much sense unless you're following interesting people. If you find yourself wandering around the site, **wondering what everyone's so excited about and where all the people are,** it's time to get suggestions for people to follow.

Click Find People, and then head to the Suggested Users tab. There you'll find a beefy list of people and companies that Twitter finds interesting. After you've followed a few, your account page will look like this—with incoming messages from the people you're now following.

In Chapter 2, we describe some good third-party tools you can use to find great followees.

Turning Twitter off and on: device notifications

- **ON:** turns ALL phone notifications on.
- **OFF:** turns ALL phone notifications off.
- **STOP, QUIT:** stops all messages to your phone immediately

- **ON username:** turns on notifications for a specific person on your phone. For example, ON alissa.
- **OFF username:** turns off notifications for a specific person on your phone. For example, OFF blaine.

- **FOLLOW username:** this command allows you to start receiving notifications for a specific person on your phone. Example: follow jeremy
- **LEAVE username:** this command allows you to stop receiving notifications for a specific person on your phone. Example: leave benfu

Twitter from the road

Part of Twitter's beauty is that you can send and receive messages from your desktop *and* from your mobile phone—meaning Twitter goes where you go. Many people find that because their status changes a lot when they're out and about, SMS **updates on the phone are a natural fit.**

To set up your phone for sending, head to Settings → Devices and type in your phone number. If you want to receive messages on your phone, too, make sure you select the little box for this option. Your mobile carrier will charge you standard text-messaging rates for Twitter updates, so keep an eye on volume. (As we describe in Chapter 5, you can specify which of your followees' messages you get on your phone.)

To post a message from your phone in the US, use the code 40404. In Canada, use 21212. In the UK, Vodafone users can text to the local UK Vodafone short code 86444; people on all other UK carriers should use +44 7624 801423. In Sweden, use: +46 737 494222. In Germany, use +49 17 6888 50505. Anywhere else, use +44 7624 801423.

To help make your phone use more efficient, Twitter has created a handful of commands you can use. Those shown here are from the Twitter help pages. For a complete list, head to http://help.twitter.com → Getting Started → The Official Twitter Text Commands.

Of course, if you use an iPhone or BlackBerry, you can skip the SMS geekery by using one of the sleek mobile Twitter clients described in Chapter 2. Not only are they easier and more fun, they also save you SMS charges.

This unusually helpful sentence, including all of the spaces and all of the punctuation, is precisely one hundred and forty characters long.

Test-drive the 140-character limit

One hundred forty characters is about the length of a headline. To get a sense of what that feels like, type up a message in the "What are you doing?" box. As you type, the Twitter website counts down your remaining characters (look just above the box where you're typing). If you're on a phone, remember to use just 140 of the 160 characters in your outgoing texts.

As you can see here, **140 characters is approximately a sentence, maybe two.** Bear in mind that your 140 characters includes spaces.

By the way, posts on Twitter are capped at 140 characters for a reason: text messages on your phone are limited to just 160 characters. Twitter takes that base and reserves 20 characters for usernames, leaving you with a tidy 140.

twitter tip

Wondering what to twitter about? In the Introduction and throughout the rest of the book, we offer ideas and examples of great things to post. Or look on Twitter, find somebody whose messages you like, and then mimic his style and get inspiration from his topics.

Home Profile Find People Settings Help Sign out

Teaching tomorrow, then heading to
PHX to give a Twitter talk @ BSeC, then
on to NJ + NY for a few days. As per
usual: shoe dilemmas abound

9:43 PM Apr 4th from twhirl

SarahM
Sarah Milstein

Home Profile Find People Settings Help Sign out

NYC organ damaged in 9/11 to be
played today 1st time since attacks
http://twurl.nl/x4mc7p (& more organ
stuff - http://twurl.nl/6lmwj0)

about 6 hours ago from TweetDeck

deanmeistr
Dean Meyers

Home Profile Find People Settings Help Sign out

WE LOVE   WE LOVE
HAVING   HAVING   HAVING

Today, so far: Beth's artist talk,
interview w/a photo mag + plotting
May w. @jteuton: NEXT, @20x200
Chicago Confab + Christian Chaize @
jbg

40 minutes ago from TweetDeck

jenbee
Jen Bekman

WE LOVE   WE LOVE   WE LOVE

Trim messages that are too long

If your message bulges above 140 characters, **here are a few common tricks you can use to tighten them up** (we discuss URL shorteners later in this chapter):

1. Use a plus sign (+) instead of "and"

2. Leave out periods and other punctuation, especially at the end of a sentence

3. Use common and not-so-common abbreviations where the meaning is clear

4. Omit "I" and perhaps the verb "to be"

5. Use numerals instead of writing out the numbers

6. Lotta times, you can cut the first few words of a sentence

twitter tip

If you need help shrinking your prose down to 140 characters, try **140it** (http://140it.com), which uses common cutting conventions to whittle down potential posts.

bit.ly Shorten, share, and track your links

Home | Tools | Search | Blog

Enter Web Address (URL) Here

http://searchengineland.com/analysis-which-url-shortening-service-should-you-use-17204#choices

Optional Custom Name

Shorten

bit.ly Shorten, share, and track your links

Home | Tools | Search | Blog

Shortened URL

http://bit.ly/G0hzU   Copy   Info   Shorten Another

Source: http://searchengineland.com/analysis-which-url-s...

The secret to linking in Twitter

The instant you try to post a link on Twitter, you realize that **most URLs don't come close to fitting in your 140-character limit—especially if you've actually said anything in the message.** The good news is that you can get help from an array of URL shorteners, services that take a URL and shrink it down to somewhere between 11 and approximately 30 characters.

If you post a link from the Twitter website or your phone, Twitter itself will automatically use TinyURL to shorten your link. That's handy, but a few other services are built in the major Twitter clients (described in Chapter 2) and offer more sophisticated shortening features.

Two of our favorites are **Bit.ly** (http://bit.ly), which lets you customize short URLs and track click-throughs, and **Is.gd** (http://is.gd), which doesn't offer tracking but does make your URLs really, really short.

For a service that hints at the underlying domain (for example, http://oreilly.twi.bz/b), try **Twi.bz** (http://twi.bz).

Name Tim O'Reilly
Location Sebastopol, CA
Web http://radar.orei...
Bio Founder and CEO, O'Reilly
Media. Watching the alpha
geeks, sharing their stories,
helping the future unfold.

514	236,165	6,257
following	followers	updates

Name Sarah Milstein
Location SF Bay Area & NYC
Web http://sarahmilst...
Bio Writer/speaker/consultant.
Making connections, eating
lunch. (For great Twitter
resources, see
@TweetReport, which I
maintain.)
sarah.milstein@gmail.com

199	7,406	4,053
following	followers	updates

Figure out how many people to follow

Everyone has a different theory of how many people you should follow. Some say 50 is the optimal number. Others argue that 100 is perfect. A lot of people follow 150 to 300. Many believe you should follow everybody who follows you.

Given the range of opinions, **you should feel confident in doing whatever works best for you.** To figure that out, try following 40 or 100 people for a few weeks, and see how that works. Follow more or unfollow people as you see fit (in Chapter 3, we talk about the perceived politics of unfollowing; but in a nutshell, we say don't sweat it).

If you want to filter or group your incoming messages in order to keep a closer eye on just a few followees, we give tips for that in Chapters 2 and 5.

twitter tip

Businesses on Twitter have different issues than individuals about whom to follow. In Chapter 6, we talk about corporate considerations.

#hashtags

search

What's happening right now on twitter

#followfriday
7,705
RT @AlexKaris : How #followfriday works
http://TwitPWR.com/a6L/ <RT this> *2 minutes ago*

Past 6 hours

#tcot
528
For #golf fans and fans of #Tiger (Tiger Woods), he is now on the live streaming feed @ the #masters dot com #-golf #pga #TCOT #RUSH #SGP *4 minutes ago*

Past 6 hours

#pman
391
pe cei care incearca sa istige , prin folosirea metodelor de dezinformare conforma manualelor SIS , ignorati ca asta'i doare #pman *3 minutes ago*

Past 6 hours

#fb
269
Decided to cut xtown by cutting across centrL park #fb *6 minutes ago*

Past 6 hours

#follow
165
@Twitter_Tips @michaelemlong @PaulaBrett .. Get down and Tweet dirty on #Follow Friday! *4 minutes ago*

Past 6 hours

#module09
158
And we are back - @scottmonty takes the stage. #module09 *3 minutes ago*

Past 6 hours

Join a conversation: the hashtag (#) demystified

People new to Twitter find hashtags among the most confusing aspects of the system. But it's one of the most useful conventions, and it's **actually a simple idea, worth getting your head around.**

Because there's no way on Twitter to categorize a message or to say, "All these messages are about the same event," users created an ad hoc solution: When somebody wants to designate related messages, they come up with a short term and prefix it with the # symbol. (In programmer-speak, that symbol is a hash mark, and the term is a tag; thus "hashtag.") Then others add the hashtag to messages about that topic.

Hashtags serve many purposes. Perhaps the most common is denoting events, like Module Midwest Digital Conference (#module09, shown in this shot from Hashtags.org). But increasingly popular are tags that signify messages from a group of people, like #tcot, shown here, which stands for "top conservatives on Twitter." Twitter memes also show up often, like #FollowFriday, shown here and described in Chapter 4 (the #follow tag is a variation). The #fb tag here is interesting: it's part of the way you can cross-post messages to Facebook, described in Chapter 5. In Chapter 3, we offer ideas on using hashtags yourself.

To see messages categorized with a hashtag, head to **Twitter search** (http://search.twitter.com, detailed in Chapter 2) and run a query for your term. **Hashtags.org** (http://hashtags.org) also shows popular hashtags and some stats on their usage. **Tagalus** (http://tagal.us) and **What the Trend** (http://whatthetrend.com, described in Chapter 2) can help you figure out what a particular hashtag is about.

Home   Profile   Find People   Settings   Help   Sign out

twitter

Priceless quote at the end of this article about Intellipedia. Too long for a tweet, alas. http://bit.ly/JY2U via Ross Stapleton-Gray

11:43 AM Mar 21st from twhirl

timoreilly
Tim O'Reilly

Key Twitter jargon: tweet

A lot of Twitter conventions and jargon—perhaps most—have **come from users rather than from the company.** The language around the service is no exception, and "tweet" is a perfect example.

A term created by users, "tweet" refers to a single Twitter post. The term is also sometimes used as a verb, as in, "We're live-tweeting the four-hour wait at Pizzeria Bianco."

Trivia: Twitter itself didn't incorporate the term "tweet" into its site until three years after the service started.

twitter

What are you doing?

140

|

Latest: @alleytrocre Re speaker, STAT: Hahahahahah! 13 minutes ago

update

Mentions of @SarahM

Read about changes to Replies

crowdvine RT @sarahm: Very smart, useful post by @heymarci:
The Seven Deadly Sins of Networking (and how to avoid them)
http://tinyurl.com/d98pv3
less than 20 seconds ago from web

MobileMrktg @SarahM Myth busted? ;)
41 minutes ago from TweetDeck in reply to SarahM

alleytrocre @SarahM we need a speaker STAT LOL
about 1 hour ago from web in reply to SarahM

SarahM

109 | 210 | 4,039
following | followers | updates

Tweet Deck
n. a powerful dashboard for
Twitter and more.

Home

@SarahM

Direct Messages   239

Favorites

Everyone

Following

Key Twitter jargon: @messages

In the beginning, there was no way to send a message to anybody else on Twitter. You just used the system for posting status updates. But pretty quickly, **people found that they wanted to hold conversations on Twitter, and public conversation at that.** So users started adding the @ symbol to the beginning of account names as a way to send a public message or refer to somebody on Twitter.

After a while, Twitter itself incorporated the convention and took it a very useful step further: now, an @ symbol followed by an account name is a link to that account page. Thus @messages—also sometimes called @mentions or @replies—are a key piece of networking on Twitter, helping you discover new people.

To see @messages to you or mentioning you, head to your Twitter home page and look along the right side for the tab that says *@YourAccountName*.

twitter tip

In Chapter 4, we explain why, when you want everyone who follows you to see a message, you shouldn't start it with the @ symbol.

Key Twitter jargon: retweet

"Retweeting" is one of the silliest-sounding terms floating around Twitter. But don't be fooled, because it's also **one of the most important.**

Retweeting is simply the act of reposting somebody else's cool or insightful or helpful tweet and giving them credit. Retweets (or RTs) help important messages work their way around Twitter. They also suggest esteem: when you RT somebody else, you implicitly say, "I respect you and your message." Indeed, as we discuss in Chapter 2, being retweeted a lot can be a sign of influence on Twitter.

In addition, as we describe on the last page, when you use the @ symbol to refer to somebody else on Twitter—always part of a retweet—you automatically create a link to his account. Retweeting is thus part of the network system on Twitter, and it's not unlike bloggers' linking to another blog.

In Chapter 3, we give you a bevy of tips on retweeting clearly and classily.

Direct message RyanSeacrest:

d RyanSeacrest Love the show this year, but can't you do something about Simon's hair?

Latest: Folks, we just followed back a bunch of you. We'll be thrilled if nobody DMs us a "Thx for the follow!" Why? It's spam: htt... 10 minutes ago

send

Key Twitter jargon: DM

Although messages on Twitter are public by default, **the system does have a private message option.** Private notes on Twitter are called "direct messages," or DMs, and they fit the usual 140-character mold. The tricky part is that in order for you to send a DM, the recipient has to be following you. Confusingly, if you're following somebody who isn't following you, he *can* DM you.

On the Twitter website, you can send a DM from the Direct Messages tab on the right side of your account page. From your Twitter home page, or from your phone, you can send a DM by starting a message with the letter "d" followed by the account name you want to reach (skip the @ symbol), and then your message. The whole package looks like the example here.

twitter tip

Twitter has a feature that sends an email when somebody DMs you (look under Settings → Notices). It's a good idea to leave that on because, frankly, the emails are pretty reliable, and Twitter sometimes fails to deliver DMs via the other channels.

Create a tweetup. Invite your tweeple!

Invite | Who is going? (11) | Comments (0) | Tweets (30) | Embed

Another tweetup in the making...

@legaladmin invites you to:

Seattle Legal Bloggers (#sealegalblog)

Seattle Legal Blogging community UNITE! Legal blogger?
Interested in starting? Want to know legal bloggers? Join us!

Where?
Spitfire

When?   What time?
Apr 21, 2009   5:30 - 7:30pm

Key Twitter jargon: tweetup

Preplanned or spontaneous, a "tweetup" is an in-person gathering organized largely via Twitter. Whether social, professional or for a cause, **a tweetup often brings together people who previously knew each other only on Twitter.** Such events are very satisfying, as the face-to-face meetings can spark new connections.

Even better, because messages on Twitter are public, tweetups can draw a mix of people who don't already know each other (even on Twitter), generating new connections.

For help organizing a tweetup, try **Twtvite** (http://twtvite.com), shown here.

twitter tip
Of course, part of the charm in a tweetup is that you can all twitter about the event as it transpires. If you're feeling fancy, designate a hashtag, described earlier in this chapter, to group everyone's messages.

Twitter is over capacity.

Too many tweets! Please wait a moment and try again.

52

Twitter jargon: Fail Whale

Twitter has grown quickly. As a consequence of that success, the service conks out often. How often? Frequently enough to have **its own logo for downtime.** Infamously known as the "Fail Whale," it appears on the screen when Twitter is over capacity.

Little-known fact: the whale was designed by Yiying Lu, who posted it to iStockPhoto, where Twitter co-founder Biz Stone came across it. Lu has since taken the image down from iStockPhoto, but you can see more of her illustrations at http://yiyinglu.com.

Why I Love Twitter

Sat Nov 29 2008

by Tim O'Reilly | comments: 95   listen ◀

If you care what I think, you know that Twitter is just about the best way to learn 🖼what I'm paying attention to. I pass along tidbits of O'Reilly news, interesting reading from mailing lists and blogs I follow, and of course, tidbits from the twitterers I'm following. These are all the things I could never find time to put on my blog, but that I spray via email like a firehose at editors, conference planners, and researchers within O'Reilly. A lot of my job is, as we say, "redistributing the future" - following interesting people, and passing on what I learn to others. And twitter is an awesome tool for doing just that.

Like a lot of people, I tried out Twitter early on, but didn't stick to it.
conversation was personal, and I didn't have time for it. I came back

listeners, I thought I'd better oblige. (There are now close to 16,000.) I soon realized that Twitter has grown up to become a critical business tool, ideal for following the latest news, tracking the ideas and

Try it for three weeks or your money back—guaranteed!

People often say that they dip into Twitter once or twice and don't get it. Which is understandable since the real value of Twitter becomes evident only after you've followed a few accounts for a while and have absorbed their rhythms.

If you're having trouble seeing what all the fuss is about, try this tactic: follow at least a few promising accounts, and then for three weeks, log into Twitter daily (ideally using one of the life-changing programs we describe in Chapter 2), catch up on messages and click around for five to ten minutes. Every few days, make sure to check the trending topics (described in Chapter 2). Finally, spend 30 minutes one day running a few searches (also described in Chapter 2) to see what you can learn from the discussions on Twitter.

At the end of three weeks, you'll have spent five hours total giving a fair shake to the most important new communications tool we've seen since email. (If it still doesn't work for you, pass this book along to a friend.)

Twitter Support

HOME   SUBMIT A REQUEST   CHECK YOUR EXISTING REQUESTS

Help Resources

Getting Started (33)
Find answers to common questions!

Twitter Announcements and Features! (4)
When a new feature is launched or something you're used to changes, find out about it here!

Trouble Shooting (17)
Having problems? Check out some of our most common issues and what to do about them

Known Issues (29)
Find updates about open bugs and currently known issues. Click the 'subscribe' link to receive email updates

Help Resources

- Getting Started (33)
- Twitter Announcements and Features! (4)
- Trouble Shooting (17)
- Known Issues (29)
- Terms of Service and Rules policies (11)

Search

[   ]

[(All)   ▼]

[Search]

Get help from Twitter

Twitter has a few dozen employees and millions of users. Given that ratio, the company does a remarkable job of providing support. Here are their **primary help channels:**

1. Twitter's help pages (http://help.twitter.com) are pretty clear and comprehensive. They include good explanations, descriptions of known problems, troubleshooting tips and a place to file or check on the status of a support request.

2. If you've encountered a spammer, you can **send a message to @spam.** In Chapter 3, we give details on the process.

3. Get Satisfaction hosts forums where people discuss Twitter issues: http://getsatisfaction.com/twitter.

CHAPTER 2 | Listen In

Twitter gives you two superhero strengths everyone wants: the power to read people's thoughts and the ability to overhear conversations as if you were a fly on the wall.

To get those bionic senses, you need the right tools and a few search skills. In this chapter, we give you a guided tour of essential listening on Twitter—the who, what, where, why and how.

 "organic food" | Search

Realtime results for **"organic food"**

0.48 seconds

 go2foodnews: A thoughtful piece from Mark Bittman about why good food should trump **organic food**: http://eaturl.info/hawx @aliciak

about 1 hour ago from *web* · Reply · View Tweet

 CNNMoney: Video: Growing an **organic food** empire: The founders of Amy's Kitchen went from testing recipes in their ki... http://tinyurl.com/c7z7l5 (expand)

about 1 hour ago from *twitterfeed* · Reply · View Tweet

 SummerTomato: New Post: Is **Organic Food** Really Better? http://bit.ly/gZ2Xq (expand)

about 1 hour ago from *TweetDeck* · Reply · View Tweet

 thegoodhuman: RT @farmfed The goal is not to eat **organic food**, but to eat food that is better for our health and planet http://ow.ly/1iyU Amen to that.

about 2 hours ago from *web* · Reply · View Tweet

Use Twitter Search

Because people twitter about the things they do, encounter, read and think, the site has been described as a sentiment machine. Truly, **it's a goldmine of ideas, feelings and conversations.**

To become a fly on the wall, head to Twitter's search feature, which lives on its own page: **http://search.twitter.com.** Here you can see that a search for the phrase "organic food" brings up a slew of results with people discussing articles about the topic.

As people post to Twitter, their messages get added to the search site in *real time*. Twitter lets you know fresh updates are available by posting a little message at the top of your results screen, complete with a Refresh link.

twitter tip

You can make Twitter search much more powerful by using a few simple search tricks. To search for a phrase, put quotes around it, as we do here. To remove a search term, put the minus sign (-) in front of it. To search for either of two terms, put the word "or" between them.

See what's happening — *right now.*

```
|
```

Advanced Search

Search

Trending topics: Earth Hour, ShamWow, Syracuse, #latelate, #earthhour, Aliens, Louisville, TGiF, #bcc2, NCAA

Keep on an eye on hot topics

To make your eavesdropping easier, Twitter search has a feature called trending topics. It lists the **top ten most popular words or phrases being twittered about at any given moment.**

Because Twitter refreshes this list regularly, the trending topics reflect the things people are most intensely interested in. It often reveals breaking news before mainstream media outlets begin reporting (the November terrorist attacks in Mumbai and a number of earthquakes trended almost instantly). And it includes durable subjects that people can't get enough of (Sarah Palin was on the list for months).

Here you can see that at the moment, people are talking about Earth Hour (the global campaign to have people turn off their lights for a specified hour), the ShamWow pitchman scandal, the NCAA March Madness tournament, the release of the movie *Monsters vs. Aliens* and other juicy topics. (In Chapters 1 and 3, we discuss hashtags, or terms preceded by the # symbol, which often appear among the trending topics.)

Incidentally, on search results pages, the trending topics appear on the right side of your screen.

What the Trend?

Find out what's trending on Twitter and why. For each trend, we give you a quick explanation of WHY it's trending (these blurbs are edited by you!) You can also see the latest tweets, Flickr photos and news stories.

Ciroc
Last trend 2 minutes ago
First trend 12 minutes ago

Why is Ciroc trending? Be the first to explain why!

#todaysmama
Last trend 2 minutes ago
First trend 12 minutes ago

Why is #todaysmama trending? Be the first to explain why!

#bcc2
Last trend 2 minutes ago
First trend about an hour ago

Why is #bcc2 trending? Barcamp Canberra 2 is happening right now!
http://www.barcamp.org/BarCampCanberra

ShamWow
Last trend 2 minutes ago
First trend about 3 hours ago

Why is ShamWow trending? ShamWow spokesman got arrested for assault. He picked up a hooker and she bit his toungue and wouldn't let go so he started punching her in the face. http://www.tmz.com/2009/03/27/shamwow-pitchman-beats-hooker-to-the-punch/

Four cool tools for tracking trends: #1

The trending topics are all well and good when you can tell what they're about (*Watchmen*, *Grey's Anatomy*, Inauguration). But **what about the cryptic terms?** (BOC, #bcc2, Ben.)

Enter **What the Trend** (http://whatthetrend.com), which lists trending topics, along with a brief description of each. If there's no explanation yet for a topic, the site invites you to add one, assuming someone will know the story. You can also edit existing topics.

twitter tip

If you're running a group chat or event whose hashtag trends on Twitter, jump over to What the Trend to make sure there's accurate info listed.

twitter

TweetingTrends

Follow

New Twitter Trend : #earthquake http://minurl.org/CaFW
11:48 PM Apr 5th from web

New Twitter Trend : L'Aquila http://minurl.org/uotS
11:28 PM Apr 5th from web

New Twitter Trend : Goonies http://minurl.org/886g
10:02 PM Apr 5th from web

New Twitter Trend : ACMu2019s http://minurl.org/Qzmy
10:02 PM Apr 5th from web

New Twitter Trend : Italy http://minurl.org/spay
9:27 PM Apr 5th from web

Updates

Favorites

Actions
block TweetingTrends

RSS feed of TweetingTrends's
updates

Four cool tools for tracking trends: #2

The list of **trending topics on Twitter search provides a window into the hive mind.** But you can't spend 24 hours a day staring into it to make sure you're catching all the important events. On the next couple of pages, we show you three tools to keep you abreast of the buzz.

Here's a simple way to get the word: On Twitter, just follow **Tweeting Trends** (@TweetingTrends), which posts a message whenever a new topic hits the list.

twitter tip

If you prefer, you can get an RSS feed of the Tweeting Trends messages. On its Twitter account page, just look on the right-hand side for the RSS icon and link.
(Of course, that works for any account on Twitter!)

TWITSCOOP
WHAT'S HOT ON TWITTER RIGHT NOW!
HOME
TWEET THIS CLOUD!
WIDGETS
FOLLOW US ON TWITTER
ABOUT
SHARE
Buzzing right now
14:02
age amanda aniston arrive atlanta babies bee
board british brooklyn chapter chinese contract corporate cure def
doc dow eastenders epenis epic essay fairy fantasy
financial fish gadget gain gorgeous grrr guessing harvey
henry heroes honor hung idk jennifer jonas kenny links linux
mayer national nite notes november nyt
obsession oprah plant points powers
refuse relationship revenue rise serve ship spin spirit
states steve stronger suit surgery tedxusc united
women
You can input a twitter username or keywords in the search box to track a conversation, topic or conference. The results will auto-refresh every 20 seconds:
search
Hot trends
dow
drobo
lance armstrong race
curt schilling
lauer matt deer
mike
vodafone
tar heel short
redoubt eruption avo
hcsm

Four cool tools for tracking trends: #3

TwitScoop (http://twitscoop.com) shows a tag cloud of terms that are becoming increasingly popular on Twitter at the moment. (In a tag cloud, the bigger the word, the more often it's been mentioned.) **It's handy for discovering topics before they hit the official trending list.**

As you can see here, under "Buzzing right now," Aniston is a growing topic. At the time of this screenshot, it hadn't yet made it to Twitter's trending topics. But it did arrive shortly after we took this picture.

twitter tip

To get a chart of the recent activity around a single term or Twitter user, use the search box on the right side of the TwitScoop page.

twopular beta

trends on **twitter** aggregator

trends on **twitter** right now

ExecTweets   Lance Armstrong   At&t   Twilight   #musicmonday   #TEDxUSC   #SxSW   Car

2 hours	8 hours	day	week	month	ever since

trends on **twitter** in the last two hours

→ Lance Armstrong 2.00	ts ℕ Ⲩ	→ Twilight 2.00	ts ℕ Ⲩ → A
→ #SxSW 2.00	ts ℕ Ⲩ	→ #musicmonday 2.00	ts ℕ Ⲩ → E
→ #mwrc09 1.25	ts ℕ Ⲩ	↓ AIG 1.05	ts ℕ Ⲩ ↓ T
↓ #baltimoremd 1.00	ts ℕ Ⲩ	↗ RSS Management 0.55	ts ℕ Ⲩ ↗ #
↑ Canadian 0.30	ts ℕ Ⲩ	↑ iPhone 0.30	ts ℕ Ⲩ ↗ A

Four cool tools for tracking trends: #4

Twopular (http://twopular.com) shows the trending topics for the last two hours, eight hours, day, week, month and "ever since." (The "ever since" category lists the most popular trends on Twitter since Twopular started keeping track in December 2008.)

It's handy not only because it **gives you snapshots over time,** but also because it has little icons telling you whether a topic was climbing, falling or staying in place at any given time.

twitter tip

Each entry in the Twopular lists has three icons next to it, one each for Twitter search, Google news and Yahoo! News. Click the appropriate icon to get fresh results for that topic.

| to:The_Real_shaq near:"portland or" within:1 | Search |

Realtime results for **to:The_Real_shaq**
near:"portland or" within:100mi ?   5.76 seconds

bwwjr: @THE_REAL_SHAQ yo! u got any extra tix to the game in PDX Thursday?
The game is SOLD OUT! and i need to see Shaq Kill Oden in the paint!
Aloha, OR
about 5 hours ago from *web* · Reply · View Tweet

true2lif: @THE_REAL_SHAQ Dairy Queen aint cheating, thats called throwin in the
towel. lol... For real, Can you share you diet with a brotha???
Hillsboro, Oregon
4 days ago from *web* · Reply · View Tweet

CosmicCharlie97: @THE_REAL_SHAQ Pick me up a Dilly Bar?
Portland, Oregon
4 days ago from *web* · Reply · View Tweet

xBitterblossomx: @THE_REAL_SHAQ gonna be some where for a while? The big
snickers with some everlasting nugget? Hungry why wait ?
PDX
4 days ago from *TwitterFon* · Reply · View Tweet

Solumus: @the_real_shaq seriously, do you sleep?
iPhone: 44.860161,-123.205490
4 days ago from *Tweetie* · Reply · View Tweet

mike_ace: @THE_REAL_SHAQ how do you use a blackberry with hands so big - is
it a foot wide?
Portland, OR

Take advantage of advanced search

Twitter's **advanced search is one of the best—and most underused—parts of the service.** To find it, head to http://search.twitter.com and look near the search box for the Advanced Search link, or just go right to http://search.twitter.com/advanced.

When you click through, you'll get a form that looks like any old advanced search. But don't be fooled. It actually has several very cool options that you won't find in almost any other search—and they make Twitter search ultra-powerful.

Although these fields may look mundane, don't miss: **1) People**, **2) Places**, **3) Attitudes** (which includes the very useful option "Asking a question?") and **4) Containing links.** The search results shown here are from people near Portland, Oregon who have asked Shaquille O'Neal a question.

twitter tip

The date search goes back just three months. If you need older search results, try a Google search in which you include "site:twitter.com" or "site:twitter.com/AnyAccountName" plus your search terms (but without the quotes).

twitter

kaiser -chiefs -rolls | Search

Realtime results for **kaiser -chiefs -rolls**

0.04 seconds

 grindcrank: In Anlehnung an Roland **Kaiser** die ganze Nacht lang das Wort "Begehren" buchstabiert. War eher langweilig.

about 1 hour ago · Reply · View Tweet

 kweenie: Another night with Lucy and **Kaiser**. I love puppy kisses!

about 1 hour ago · Reply · View Tweet

 guaitaaa: Encara que un altre dia **Kaiser**!!!

about 2 hours ago · Reply · View Tweet

 suitablegirl: is @ **Kaiser** NorCal, which is stymied by obv incorrect price the "Mid-Atlantic" region gave them. Home region my ASS. Thx for nothing, DC.

about 2 hours ago · Reply · View Tweet

 drmabuse: New Podcast! The Bat Segundo Show #264 (Veteran DC journalist Robert G. **Kaiser**) http://tinyurl.com/cbbxe4 (expand)

about 2 hours ago · Reply · View Tweet

 vacatures_15: Full-Time RN Clinical Practice Consultant: CA-Canyon-94516, DEPARTMENT: **Kaiser** Foundation Health Plan, Regional .. http://tinyurl.com /cs5p95 (expand)

about 2 hours ago · Reply · View Tweet

74

Four important things to search for

If you want really useful search results from Twitter, you have to spend some time playing with the advanced search options to figure out the relevant terms and topics people are talking about. Here are four topics to get you started:

Your name. It may be known as a "vanity search," but keeping an eye on what people say about you is a smart idea. (Don't forget that putting quotes around your name can help refine the results. Search for *"Jane Doe"* instead of *Jane Doe*.)

Your Twitter account name. Don't miss messages to or about you.

Your company, brand or product. Peek into the minds of customers, competitors, journalists and other key constituents. If you're a local business, use the advanced search "Location" option to narrow down results. Also, if your company name is common, use the minus sign to weed out inappropriate results. For instance, if you work for Kaiser Permanente, search for *Kaiser -Chiefs* to make sure messages about the band don't overwhelm your results. (Here, a targeted search yields some relevant results.)

Your competitors. Get market intel and ideas. (Chapter 6 offers more ideas for business-related searching.)

Yanks OR Yankees OR NYY	Jeter
↓ anywhere ↓ 🔊	↓ anywhere ↓ 🔊

 waiting for yankees game, in like 1 &1/2 hrs. Go Yankees!
molleeh [Reply] [Retweet] [Profile] · **14:18**

 ...overheard "is that derek Jeter?"
pamelaspunch [Reply] [Retweet] [Profile] · **13:31**

 @brittxojonas =p i hate the yankees
issa123 [Reply] [Retweet] [Profile] · **14:17**

 RT @YESNetwork: Tonight's lineup: Jeter SS, Damon LF, Swisher 1B, Posada C, Nady RF, Cano 2B, Matsui DH, Ransom 3B, Cabrera CF
proctorsarm [Reply] [Retweet] [Profile] · **13:11**

 @miss_holloway end-o-week. be careful Manny'll break ya heart. ask the yankees.
johnHlang [Reply] [Retweet] [Profile] · **14:16**

 Tonight's lineup: Jeter SS, Damon LF, Swisher 1B, Posada C, Nady RF, Cano 2B, Matsui DH, Ransom 3B, Cabrera CF
YESNetwork [Reply] [Retweet] [Profile] · **13:09**

 New #Yankees Blog: Game 7: Yankees at Rays: New York Yankees (3-3) Tampa Bay Rays (3-3) Derek ..
http://tinyurl.com/cdx2vb
proctorsarm [Reply] [Retweet] [Profile] · **14:15**

 YANKEES: Game 7: Yankees at Rays (RIP Harry Kalas): YANKEES (3-3) Jeter SS Damon LF Swisher 1B Posada C..
http://tinyurl.com/dewg9h
LoHud [Reply] [Retweet] [Profile] · **13:07**

 the show in st pete is going to be NUTS tmrw bc it's also the Rays home opener... and it's against the Yankees.
teammegan [Reply] [Retweet] [Profile] · **14:15**

 2007 Elements Baseball Box Break! Derek Jeter Mojo!: None Author: GirdironKing2009 Keywords:.. http://ad.vu/c3z4
derek_jeter [Reply] [Retweet] [Profile] · **13:06**

 Last year a constrction worker tried to curse the Yankees by planting a Red Sox jersey in the new stadium! It was found and removed, (cont...
insanezane [Reply] [Retweet] [Profile] · **14:14**

 still sooooo jealous that jacki, kim & heather met & got a pic w/ DEREK JETER this wknd!! lucky ducks!!!
joleneh3 [Reply] [Retweet] [Profile] · **12:59**

 APRIL 25TH RED SOX VS. YANKEES YANKEES R GOING DOWN
jb4eva3njk [Reply] [Retweet] [Profile] · **14:13**

 http://twitpic.com/39qhj - Jeter, that's not ur air mattress! You can't chew ur bone on there-get off! lol
DJLysaD [Reply] [Retweet] [Profile] · **10:50**

Advance your advanced search

When you want to see what people are saying about several topics at once, and you want to watch the conversations in real-time, try a service like **TweetGrid** (http://tweetgrid.com) or **Monitter** (http://monitter.com), shown here.

They're useful not only for seeing what people are saying, but also for getting **a sense of the speed and volume of tweets on different topics.**

If you find yourself keeping an eye on the same searches every day, consider using Twitter via a client like Twhirl or TweetDeck, which lets you easily save and see searches. We describe third-party programs later in this chapter.

twitter tip

For services that let you include a complex query, here's an easy way to get the search string. Use Twitter's advanced search to run your query. At the top of the results page, you'll see your query converted into a search string (something like Yankees OR Yanks near:"New York, NY" within:25mi). Paste it into your current app.

Show: 10 new items - **all items** | Mark all as read | | Refresh | | Feed settings... ▾ |

B/R >> Does Economic Slump Mean a Baseball Slump?: The Yankees will be inaugurating a new stadium th.. http://tinyurl.com/d22vnv ⊙

by MLBYankees (New York Yankees)

B/R >> Does Economic Slump Mean a Baseball Slump?: The **Yankees** will be inaugurating a new stadium th.. http://tinyurl.com/d22vnv

☆ Add star Share Share with note ✉ Email ☐ Keep unread Add tags

---

2 NY Yankees vs Boston RedSox 9/27 free e-mail shipping http://tinyurl.com/dgxo89 ⊙

by NY_Yankees (New York Yankees)

2 NY **Yankees** vs Boston RedSox 9/27 free e-mail shipping http://tinyurl.com/dgxo89

☆ Add star Share Share with note ✉ Email ☐ Keep unread Add tags

---

Kei Igawa was sent to the minors and hopefully to another team before the season starts. What a terrible "talent." http://bit.ly/HLPNZ#Yanks ⊙

by rweb35 (rweb35)

Kei Igawa was sent to the minors and hopefully to another team before the season starts. What a terrible "talent." http://bit.ly/HLPNZ#Yanks

78

Track searches with RSS

So you've spent time tinkering with Twitter search, and you've figured out a few queries that bring up useful results. Do you have to head over to Twitter search every hour and type them in to see if you've got fresh messages? Of course not.

The most basic way to keep on top of searches is to **grab an RSS feed** of them. Here's a feed, shown in Google Reader, of messages about the Yankees, posted by people near New York, that contain links (and thus are likely to point out stories and pictures on the Web).

To get a feed, just run your search, and then on the results page, look in the upper-right corner for the RSS logo and the link "Feed for this query."

Of course, it works with simple queries, too, like the results for a search on your name.

« Back to Inbox | Archive | Report spam | Delete | Move to ▾ | Labels ▾ | More actions ▾

O'Reilly Media - TweetBeep Alert Inbox | ×

☆ TweetBeep.com to me   show details 11:50 AM (0 minutes ago) ↰ Reply | ▾

Hi Sarah! 50 new tweets were found from your "O'Reilly Media" alert!

Favoriten: Books That Have Shaped How I Think | O'Reilly Media
http://bit.ly/AdOI

Tuesday, March 24th at 17:59:44 · Reply · View Tweet

zweinullweb: Books That Have Shaped How I Think | O'Reilly Media
http://tinyurl.com/dcr99x

Tuesday, March 24th at 17:56:33 · Reply · View Tweet

teelook: Books That Have Shaped How I Think | O'Reilly Media
http://tinyurl.com/dcr99x

Tuesday, March 24th at 17:55:34 · Reply · View Tweet

jflinchbaugh: O'Reilly Media Open Source Conference – ITC.oscon-
Lefkowitz-2008.07.22 http://ff.im/1HlzM

Track search with email alerts

RSS is all well and good if you're the kind of geek who spends half your time in an RSS reader. But what if you don't use RSS much or don't have any idea what RSS even means? No problem. **TweetBeep** has you covered.

TweetBeep (http://tweetbeep.com) will shoot you an **email message with an hourly or daily digest of tweets** that contain your search terms. It's like Google Alerts, only for Twitter instead of the rest of the Web.

URL Search Add Search Plugin

backtweets

—Search Links on Twitter

nytimes.com   SEARCH

Examples: http://www.youtube.com, nytimes.com, twitter »

Search Results for nytimes.com *(0.508 seconds)*

Judge Orders FDA to make Plan B available to 17-YOs , ruled agency improperly bowed to political pressure from Bush **http://bit.ly/Ytug7** *3 minutes ago*

Virgotex

4 Michigan Papers to Cut Back on Print **http://tinyurl.com/cg8n74** *3 minutes ago*

slominski

Today's wonderful misuse of medical equipment: CT scans as art: **http://bit.ly/mviOw** (Love the McNuggets!) *3 minutes ago*

TheSquare

Business Update... Advertising: A Network Takes Us Out to a Ballgame **http://tinyurl.com/d3ju32 http://ff.im/-1GDPp** *3 minutes ago*

Track twittered links to your website

If you're trying to keep track of tweets that link to your website, you've got a tricky problem. Because people use URL shorteners to create links compact enough to fit in a tweet, **you can't simply search for mentions of your domain.**

Luckily, **BackTweets** (http://backtweets.com) has your back. Just type in the URL you want to track, and it pulls up a list of appropriate results. You can search for links to a domain name (like nytimes.com, as we've shown here) or to a specific page (like http://www.nytimes.com/2009/03/24/business/media/24paper.html).

To keep a regular eye on your results, grab the RSS feed for them by clicking the RSS logo at the top of the results page.

twitter tip

To get email alerts when people twitter a URL, even a shortened one, try TweetBeep, described on the previous page.

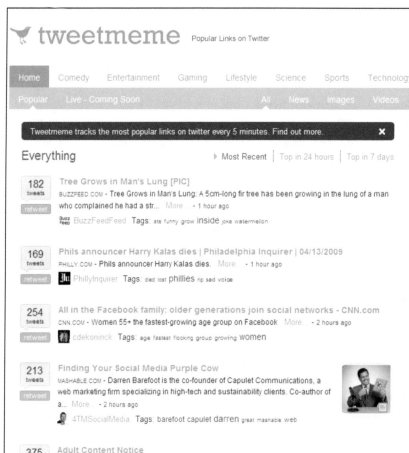

🐦 **tweetmeme**   Popular Links on Twitter

| Home | Comedy | Entertainment | Gaming | Lifestyle | Science | Sports | Technology |

Popular   Live - Coming Soon   All   News   Images   Videos

Tweetmeme tracks the most popular links on twitter every 5 minutes. Find out more.   ✕

Everything

▸ Most Recent | Top in 24 hours | Top in 7 days

182 tweets
retweet

Tree Grows in Man's Lung [PIC]
BUZZFEED.COM - Tree Grows in Man's Lung: A 5cm-long fir tree has been growing in the lung of a man who complained he had a str... More... - 1 hour ago

BuzzFeed BuzzFeedFeed   Tags: ate funny grow inside joke watermelon

169 tweets
retweet

Phils announcer Harry Kalas dies | Philadelphia Inquirer | 04/13/2009
PHILLY.COM - Phils announcer Harry Kalas dies.   More... - 1 hour ago

PhillyInquirer   Tags: died lost phillies rip sad voice

254 tweets
retweet

All in the Facebook family: older generations join social networks - CNN.com
CNN.COM - Women 55+ the fastest-growing age group on Facebook More... - 2 hours ago

cdekoninck   Tags: age fastest flocking group growing women

213 tweets
retweet

Finding Your Social Media Purple Cow
MASHABLE.COM - Darren Barefoot is the co-founder of Capulet Communications, a web marketing firm specializing in high-tech and sustainability clients. Co-author of a... More... - 2 hours ago

4TMSocialMedia   Tags: barefoot capulet darren great mashable web

375 tweets
retweet

Adult Content Notice
COMMUNITY.LIVEJOURNAL.COM - Possible culprit for starting the #amazonfail fight? More... - 3 hours ago

fredhicks   Tags: #amazonfail amazon claims credit just troll

Find out what people are reading

Because people like to twitter links to interesting things they've read, **Twitter can be your filtered news portal.** A lot of the time, the people you follow will serve up more juicy reading material than you can ingest. But if you want a snapshot of the most popular stories being passed around Twitter, these services can give you insight.

Twitt(url)y (http://twitturly.com) and **TweetMeme** (http://tweetmeme.com), shown here, both track and rank the URLs flying through the Twittersphere. They show the most popular links and how many times each has appeared in a tweet.

MicroPlaza (http://microplaza.com) not only reveals what people are paying attention to across Twitter, it also can personalize the results, showing you the most talked about links in your Twitter network.

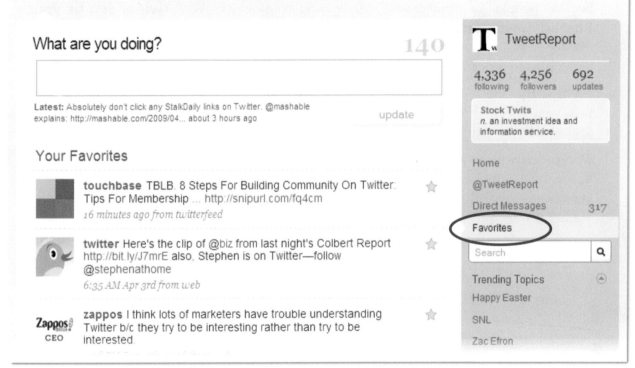

Bookmark links to read later

Twitter has a Favorites feature. While you can use it to collect funny or insightful posts, it's also **a great way to keep track of things you want to read later.** If you mouse over a message, a star appears on the right; click that to add the post to your Favorites, which appears as a list under your Favorites tab.

This trick can be especially handy when you're on the road using your phone, and you want to save a link to read later on your PC. If you're using a mobile client (discussed later in this chapter), you've almost certainly got a built-in favorite feature. If you use Twitter via SMS, you can reply to anybody's last post with the command *FAV username* to tag that message as a favorite. For more text commands, see Chapter 1.

Use a life-changing third-party program

The Twitter web interface is decent, but frankly, it's not stellar. The good news is that you have alternatives. Thanks to the way Twitter shares its data (for you geeks, that's their API), other people can and have created programs that let you access your account. And a lot of these third-party clients are much more intuitive than the Twitter website itself.

If you use Twitter more than once a week, it's time to **try a program that will make your sending, receiving and listening vastly more effective.** With just a few minutes of setup, they can take your twittering from tedious to life-changing.

There are dozens, if not hundreds, of third-party clients. On the next pages, we describe a couple of our favorites. Here we've shown PeopleBrowsr (http://peoplebrowsr.com), a browser-based program that gives you a mind-blowing range of ways to view your account.

twitter tip

All clients and some other third-party Twitter programs require that you share your Twitter password. While it's usually OK to share your Twitter username, be very careful with your password. Share it only with programs and websites that you feel are truly trustworthy.

Life-changing program #1: Twhirl

Compact and good-looking, **Twhirl sits on your desktop and delivers a stream of tweets.** Unlike the Twitter website, it doesn't require that you refresh in order to see new messages—it just flows them out to you.

On the sending side, Twhirl is strong. For each incoming message, it gives you easy options to reply, retweet, DM or mark as a favorite. It has a built-in URL-shortening feature that lets you choose the compression service. And it integrates with TwitPic, a photo-sharing site for tweets, among other services.

On the listening side, Twhirl really shines. It automatically shows you any messages that contain @*YourUserName,* and it creates Twitter search links out of hashtags. To help you understand at a glance what's coming in, it color codes the messages (here, green tells you that @*YourUserName* appears in a post). Perhaps best of all, it lets you create searches, and then it inserts the results right in your incoming stream—an incredibly efficient way to keep on top of the things that matter to you.

Before installing **Twhirl** (http://twhirl.org), you must run Adobe Air (http://www.adobe.com/products/air). That sounds intimidating, but each takes just a few minutes to download and run. Be aware that desktop web applications tend to suck up system resources over time; be sure to close and restart them every day or so.

Note: As we were going to press, Twhirl's company, Seesmic, was in the process of launching an updated version of Twhirl, Seesmic Desktop. Keep an eye out for it.

Life-changing program #2: TweetDeck

TweetDeck is one of the most popular Twitter clients. Why? Because in addition to an array of helpful receiving and sending features, it has **one outstanding property for listening:** it lets you group your incoming messages.

That means that if you follow 300 people, or 3,000, but you really only have time to keep up with 30 of them, TweetDeck can show you a column of messages from just your inner circle. You can also group messages by keyword or hashtag. Plus, it has a built-in way to see TwitScoop trends.

TweetDeck (http://tweetdeck.com) is a desktop program, and before you install it, you need to run Adobe Air (http://www.adobe.com/products/air). That sounds intimidating, but each takes just a few minutes to download and run. Be aware that desktop web applications tend to suck up system resources over time because they don't do what programmers call "automatic garbage collection." Be sure to close and restart them every day or so.

Use a great mobile client

A good deal of Twitter's appeal comes from the fact that you can **send and receive messages from anywhere you happen to be with your mobile phone.** Twitter's own mobile service, http://m.twitter.com, is fine but basic. If you want to amp up your listening on the road, try a dedicated mobile client.

For the iPhone, **Twitterific** (http://iconfactory.com/software/twitterrific/) and **Tweetie** (http://www.atebits.com/software/tweetie), shown here, are popular.

For the BlackBerry, try **TwitterBerry** (http://orangatame.com/products/twitterberry) or **TinyTwitter** (http://tinytwitter.com).

Incidentally, you don't have to run the same mobile and desktop clients. It works totally fine to run, say, Twhirl on your desktop and Twitterific on your iPhone.

Showing: **Relevant folks to check out** • <u>My Followers I am not following</u>

Good people relevant to your recent follows and tweets.

Displaying **1 - 10** of **200** (<u>See All</u>)

New
1
[x]

Follow

Say Hi

Sara Peyton / <u>sarapeyton</u>

PR Manager @ O'Reilly Media

Followed by **Tim O'Reilly**, Kathy Sierra, Nat Torkington, Brian Jepson and 22 others

Show Tweets

Show Replies

593 Following	566 Followers	0.95 Ratio

Characteristics:

Updates: 1.4 tweets a day
Links: 76%
Conversations: 48%

Info:

Location: Occidental, CA
Site: <u>http://www.oreilly.com</u>

New
2
[x]

Follow

Say Hi

hexodus / <u>hexodus</u>

currently making millions in the philosophy industry!

Followed by **dontgetcaught**, Olivia Mitchell, ETech Conference, Bert Decker and 8 others

Show Tweets

Show Replies

102 Following	1601 Followers	16 Ratio

Characteristics:

Reciprocity: Frequently replies to non-follows
Updates: 24 tweets a day

Follow smart people you don't know

You can use Twitter to stay in touch with friends and family. But **to get the most out of the service, follow at least a few people you don't already know.** They'll point out articles you wouldn't normally see. They'll give you a sense of what's important in another region, industry or social sphere. In addition, if you're using Twitter for professional reasons, following peers and thought leaders in your sector can help establish a connection.

A number of services can help you find smart, interesting people to follow. First, start on Twitter's own search site (http://search.twitter.com), look up a few terms that are important to you, and see who's sharing good ideas and links. Then take a look at searchable directories like **We Follow** (http://wefollow.com) and **Twellow** (http://twellow.com), which organize Twitterers by topic.

Finally, try a recommendation engine, like **Mr. Tweet** (http://mrtweet.net), shown here, or **Who Should I Follow?** (http://whoshouldifollow.com). Based on your Twitter activity and existing network, they'll suggest other Twitterers you might find interesting.

Incidentally, while you're surfing around these sites, add yourself!

The 100 Most Influential People in Twitter

Twitalyzer » Benchmark Your Influence in Twitter

The following table contains the 100 Most Influential people in Twitter. You can sort these fine folks by their influence, their signal-to-noise ratio, their generosity, velocity, and clout. Use the arrows below the table to page through the list and click on each user to learn more about them.

Username	Influence	Trend	Signal/Noise	Generosity	Velocity	Clout
mashable	80.2	0.0%	97.6%	1.6%	16.5	99.9
guykawasaki	79.8 ▲	2.0%	90.5%	2.0%	40.7	100.0
theonion	76.2 ▲	2.3%	94.7%	0.0%	5.1	100.0
zaibatsu	75.6 ▲	1.6%	70.0%	42.1%	100.0	97.2
mayhemstudios	72.4 ▼	-0.8%	81.4%	57.0%	100.0	100.0

Figure out who's influential on Twitter

Figuring out who's influential on Twitter looks straightforward—just see who has the most followers. But **don't be deceived:** because Twitter automatically recommends followees for new accounts, and because people can game the system, the number of followers actually tells you very little about the value or influence of an account.

Take the *New York Times'* main account, a feed of headlines from their site (@nytimes). It has hundreds of thousands of followers, making it one of the most-followed Twitterers, according to **Twitterholic** (http://twitterholic.com). But it's very rarely *retweeted*, suggesting people don't find its posts highly valuable.

Speaking of retweets—a decent measure of influence—there are sites that track who's been retweeted most frequently. The most notable are **Retweetist** (http://retweetist.com) and **Retweet Radar** (http://retweetradar.com).

It's also important to know that almost anyone on the list of top Twitterers is probably on Twitter's recommended list for new users. If you check out any of them on **TwitterCounter** (http://twittercounter.com), you'll see a really sharp spike starting the day they were added to the official list. For example, see http://twittercounter.com/timoreilly/all.

For a more nuanced approach, one that takes into account followers, retweetability and other factors, check out **Twitalyzer** (http://twitalyzer.com), shown here.

CHAPTER 3 | Hold Great Conversations

A lot of people find Twitter and think, "This is the perfect place to tell the world about myself!" After all, the site asks, "What are you doing?"

But it turns out that **Twitter isn't so much a broadcast medium as it is a discussion channel.** Indeed, the secret of social media is that it's not about you, your product or your story. It's about how you can add value to the communities that happen to include you. If you want to make a positive impact, forget about what you can get out of social media and start thinking about what you can contribute. Funnily enough, the more value you create for the community, the more value it will create for you.

In this chapter and the next, we show you how great conversationalists succeed and add value to their communities on Twitter.

Sweet. My can opener followed me back. Thanks for the add!

10 minutes ago from web

 hotdogsladies

Thanks kindly to everyone who reads, replies, and retweets us. The 3 R's. We read all of your tweets here: http://bit.ly /16Rnc0.

25 minutes ago from web

venturehacks
Venture Hacks

Get great followers

If you want tons of followers on Twitter, you're not alone. But here's a secret: a small number of great followers is much more valuable than a herd of uninterested people. Think about it this way: if you're an accountant twittering about tax tips, what's the point of having 1,000 followers if 999 of them are spam bots and war resistors who don't file taxes?

As a very practical example, when @timoreilly had 30,000 followers who'd been acquired organically, about 2,000 of them would click any given link in a tweet (measured via Bit.ly, described in Chapters 1 and 6). Now, with more than a quarter of a million followers, he gets around 4,000 clicks per tweet. Lesson? Quality followers—i.e., people who care enough to follow on their own—are worth more than a great quantity of random followers.

Drawing smart followers involves three key pieces:

1. Be interesting. The best way to become popular on Twitter is to post messages that other people want to read, retweet and respond to. In the next couple of chapters, we show how plenty of people are interesting and witty in 140 characters.

2. Be conversational. Engage with people, whether they're already following you or not. People like it. Plus, when prospective followers hit your Twitter account page, they'll see you're a friendly, thoughtful person.

3. Follow relevant people. If you follow somebody, there's a good chance she'll follow you back. Use the tips in Chapter 2 to find people who are interested in the same sort of topics you are and follow them. It's the first step in building a relationship.

Home   Find People   Help   Sign out   Trends

Search now   🔍

What are you doing?

140

|

Latest: WSJ on Twitter-related revenue...being generated by companies other than Twitter: http://is.gd/oPEw about 1 hour ago

update

Mentions of @TweetReport

winecountrydog @TweetReport woof thanx fur link to twarticle "twitter tweaks title tags." btw, the fail whale has been spotted off sonoma coast again.
about 16 hours ago from web

mingyeow @TweetReport Thanks for the nice words! Some people say thoughtful, others say confused. ;) Hope to see you soon in SF - will be at @w2e

T·w TweetReport
Profile · Settings

3,616 following   **3,487** followers   **609** updates

Exec·tweets
n. a curation of top business executives on Twitter.

Home

@TweetReport

Direct Messages   272

Favorites

Reply to your @messages

As we explain in Chapter 1, a message that starts with @*YourUserName* is a public message to you. Sometimes those messages are a friendly hello or acknowledgment. Sometimes they're a question or comment. While **Twitter messages don't carry quite as high an expectation of response as email messages do,** it's good community practice to respond to some if not all of them (usually with a message that starts @*TheirUserName*).

Oddly, it can be tough to *find* your @messages. If you use a third-party program, as described in Chapter 2, you'll probably see them readily. But if you use the Twitter website, you have to click the @*YourUserName* tab on the right side of your screen to discover the messages people have sent you. The list also includes references to @*YourUserName*. If you mouse over a message, a swoosh appears on the right; click that to respond.

twitter tip

If you receive a random @message from somebody you don't know, and it appears to be promoting something, it's probably spam. Later in this chapter, we explain how to report it.

GREAT rant by @dannysullivan:
"Google's Love For Newspapers + How
Little They Appreciate It" http://bit.ly
/3EFVaq (via @brady)

12:05 AM Apr 7th from twhirl

SarahM
Sarah Milstein

RT @gapingvoid: Definition of
Cartooning: "Using lines to think"...

3:37 PM Apr 9th from twhirl

timoreilly
Tim O'Reilly

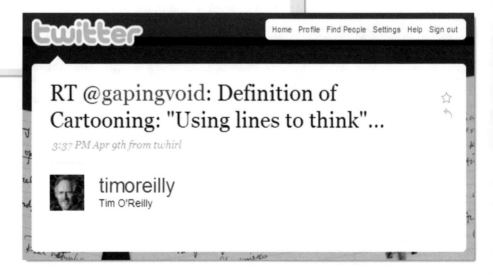

Retweet clearly and classily: Part 1

As we describe in Chapter 1, **retweeting—or reposting somebody else's useful message and giving her credit—is one of the great Twitter conventions.** Trouble is, it's surprisingly hard to do. What if adding the retweeting info bumps you over 140 characters? What if you want to edit the message? What if you want to add your own comment?

The good news is that there are no rules, so you can't Do It Wrong. The even better news is that there are a few guidelines we can share, so you don't have to reinvent the retweet every time. The examples here show you what we believe are a couple of clear and classy retweets. The next few pages give you a roadmap for creating your own.

twitter tip

In order to make yourself more retweetable, make sure your messages leave enough room for somebody to add "RT @*YourUserName*". For example, on her TweetReport account, Sarah goes no higher than 125 characters (140 – 15 for "RT @TweetReport").

Home   Profile   Find People   Settings   Help   Sign out

RT @ChronicleBooks: Too cute: The
Very Hungry Caterpillar cupcakes (via
@RainCoast books) http://ow.ly/1pEg

2 minutes ago from web

 🔒 **PatEx**
Pat Example

Home   Find People   Help   Sign out   Search

Yay: Very Hungry Caterpillar cupcakes
-- http://ow.ly/1pEg (via @jenbee
@ChronicleBooks @RaincoastBooks)

about 5 hours ago from twhirl

 SarahM
Sarah Milstein

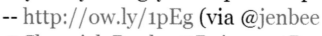

Retweet clearly and classily: Part 2

There are two primary ways people retweet:

1. "**RT** @*OriginalPosterName* yadda yadda http://someURL...." (RT stands for retweeting.)

2. "Yadda yadda yadda http://someURL (**via** @*OriginalPosterName*)."

A reasonable approach is to use RT when you're reposting a message verbatim and via when you've rewritten a message. An even better approach is to **aim for a clear message and then figure out how to credit the original Twitterer** or Twitterers.

Here you can see the original message from PatEx—itself a retweet—is starting to get complex. In her retweet, Sarah simplifies the message, adds her own editorial comment ("Yay"), and then appends the list of credits at the end.

twitter tip

See how the retweet here maintained the original shortened URL? It's good Twitter etiquette to do that when you can, because the person who first posted the message may be using a URL shortener to track click-throughs.

GREAT advice for @BarackObama on smart grid, cybersecurity, & cost-effective stimulus http://bit.ly/VDWF (via Farber's IP list)

2:22 PM Apr 10th from twhirl

timoreilly
Tim O'Reilly

RT @pahlkadot The more I read about @carlmalamud, the more I smitten I am. An open data superhero, Indiana Jones-style. [So right!]

10:10 AM Apr 10th from twhirl

timoreilly
Tim O'Reilly

When via is better than RT

Retweeting is a blessing and a curse. It can help important news spread in the blink of an eye. But it also can turn your Twitter feed into a noisy stream of redundant updates.

The problem is that, especially in many of the third-party Twitter clients, it's just too easy to retweet. You see a good link. You want to pass it on. You hit the RT button in Twhirl or Tweetdeck, then send.

Oops. Even if you've passed along something of value, it might have been even more valuable if you'd taken the time to **put your own spin on it and say why you found the link valuable.** (Of course, you'd still want to give credit for the original link.)

So pause before you retweet, and write a note that tells the world what this link means to you. Then use via to tell the world who showed you the link in the first place. (Via is also great for giving credit when you got a link from a source who isn't on Twitter.)

In an ideal world, use literal retweets only when the original phrasing is unique and a key part of what you want to pass on. A straight retweet should show the character of the person making the original posting, not just a link.

Unless, of course, it's news that's just so hot that you have to pass it on before it burns your keyboard.

Gotta agree w/@hotdogsladies:
'Organizing' your email is like
alphabetizing your recycling.

3:50 PM Apr 6th from twhirl

SarahM
Sarah Milstein

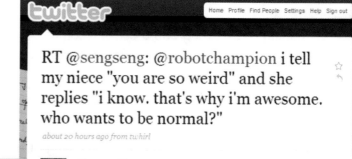

RT @sengseng: @robotchampion i tell
my niece "you are so weird" and she
replies "i know. that's why i'm awesome.
who wants to be normal?"

about 20 hours ago from twhirl

timoreilly
Tim O'Reilly

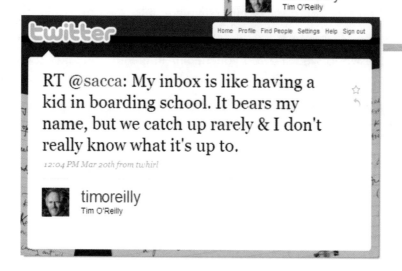

RT @sacca: My inbox is like having a
kid in boarding school. It bears my
name, but we catch up rarely & I don't
really know what it's up to.

12:04 PM Mar 20th from twhirl

timoreilly
Tim O'Reilly

What to retweet

Wondering what to retweet? Researcher Dan Zarrella (@danzarrella) has found four types of posts that are commonly retweeted:

1. How-tos and instructional stories or videos

2. News, especially breaking news

3. Warnings (like a scam or virus that's circulating)

4. Freebies and contests

Those are all pretty easy to figure out. But **Twitter is also a great medium for wit, and it's really worth retweeting a unique turn of phrase.** We've shown a few of our favorites here. For a bunch more, see http://radar.oreilly.com/2008/09/twitter-epigrams-and-repartee.html.

RT @xenijardin Doctor Popular is on our live stream right now doing yo yo tricks!!!! http://offworld.com/gdc09 [So cool!]

less than 10 seconds ago from web

 PatEx
Pat Example

Quiet heroism here: RT @larrybrilliant: Today only HBO http://bit.ly/17Sliy and YouTube http://bit.ly/WA77c streaming polio documentary.

7:40 AM Apr 7th from twhirl

timoreilly
Tim O'Reilly

Troubleshoot your retweets

To help you **retweet with confidence,** here's our FAQ for RTs.

1. What if adding the retweeting info bumps me over 140 characters? It's OK to edit down or rewrite a message. If you change it substantially, consider using the via form described on the previous page.

2. What if I want to add my own comment? No prob, people do it all the time. Here we've shown two easy ways to do it. Way 1: @PatEx adds a comment *after* the full RT. Pat uses brackets to denote the commentary. Sometimes people use a dash or a couple of slashes to create the same effect. Way 2: Tim adds a comment *before* the RT.

3. Can I change the URL to make it shorter or to track it? Because the earlier Twitterer(s) may be trying to track click-throughs on the URL they posted, it's best not to change it. But it's not a big deal if you do.

4. If the list of people who retweeted is getting too long, can I lop off some of them? Yes. Ideally give credit to the first and last person in the chain (RT @first via @last).

116

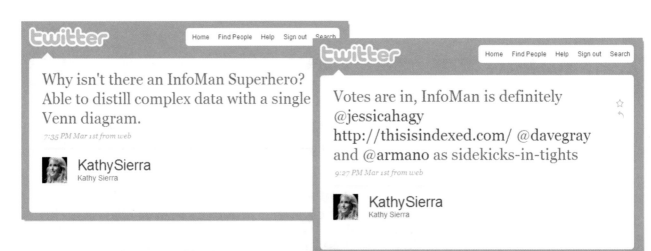

Ask questions

Who's the best flat-top barber in San Francisco?

I'm from NY. Will my iPhone incur roaming charges in Bermuda?

What kind of wine goes with tofu parmesan?

Twitter is a Q&A machine. Here's how you get in on the action: ask a question. People like to help, and Twitter lets them do so by offering just a sentence or two. So although you won't always get answers, a lot of the time you will (even if you have just a handful of followers). Twitterers are delighted to contribute their knowledge.

If you want a more formal process, or if you'd like to reach beyond your own followers, consider **TweetBrain** (http://tweetbrain.com), a Twitter-powered Q&A service.

twitter tip

To be a really good Twitter citizen, don't just ask questions, repost the best answers, too. As you can see here, closing the loop isn't hard, and it makes Twitter more valuable for everyone.

twitter Home Find People Help Sign out Search

@shellerae no idea on the
wasps...maybe this old WaccoBB post
has something useful?
http://tinyurl.com/b52vzp

10:58 AM Feb 26th from web in reply to shellerae

 terrie
Terrie Miller

twitter Home Find People Help Sign out Search

@jwikert if you've got a Mighty Mouse
(highly recommend) goto Prefs->Keybd
& Mouse->Mouse, and change the
rt-hand menu to 2ndry Button.

4:37 PM Mar 1st from twhirl in reply to jwikert

 petermeyers
Peter Meyers

Answer questions

The people you follow on Twitter may wonder where to find the best espresso in Rome, or how to train their cats from jumping up on the counters or whether PowerPoint slides can be displayed in portrait orientation. If you know the answers, don't hesitate to respond with a friendly @reply.

If you want to amp up your answering, keep an eye on http://search.twitter.com for keywords in questions you might be able to answer. (As we explain in Chapter 2, Twitter's advanced search lets you look for people asking questions.) For instance, if you're a motorcycle mechanic, you might run searches for questions containing "Harley," "Yamaha" and perhaps "broken." Though you have to use judgment about approaching strangers, **providing good info on Twitter can help you develop a positive reputation.**

twitter tip

If you run a local business and you're looking for work, use Twitter's advanced search to find people in your area asking questions you might be able to answer.

@judithsoldyess yes the problems of abundance are better than those of scarcity

8:00 AM Mar 23rd from web in reply to judithsoldyess

kanter
Beth Kanter

@pcz yes, i discovered that sitting down and having a conversation about mutual needs/concerns is the best approach

about 4 hours ago from web in reply to pcz

kanter
Beth Kanter

@riasharon how are trolls like gremlins? tell me more...advice for dealing with trolls..

9:50 PM Mar 24th from web in reply to riasharon

kanter
Beth Kanter

Send smart @replies

We see @replies like these every day:

"I hope not."

"She's my favorite!"

"Aren't we all?"

"Don't waste your money or time reading the trash he peddles!"

"Wow."

Seem meaningless to you without context? Seems that way to us, too, and these are actual @replies we've received.

The problem is that Twitter gives recipients no easy way to tell which message an individual @reply is responding to. Sometimes, if you send an @reply immediately after somebody posts an update, and she happens to get it right away, she'll know what you're referring to. But if she's amidst a flurry of twittering, even timeliness isn't fail-safe.

To ensure that your co-conversationalists know what you're talking about, do as Beth Kanter (@kanter) does here and send @replies that provide a touch of context.

You can also help by using the Twitter reply arrow (described earlier in this chapter) instead of typing in an @username. Depending on the client a reader uses, she may see a link at the bottom of your tweet, "in reply to Username." That goes to the post you were responding to.

twitter

Home Profile Find People Settings Help Sign out

@SarahM: what's with the rapid tweeting?

11:28 AM Feb 20th from txt

o_O 🔒 **kati**
Kati

twitter

Home Find People Help Sign out Search

Between @timoreilly and @SarahM, I'm not missing a minute of Web 2.0 Summit.

11:34 AM Nov 7th, 2008 from twitterrific

bgreenlee
Brad Greenlee

twitter

Home Find People Help Sign out Search

@SarahM: Thanks for tweeting Obama campaign discussion; really interesting.

12:05 PM Feb 20th from web

saragoldstein

Twitter often...but not too often

Twitter novitiates almost always wonder, "How often should I Twitter?" (Actually, Twitter pros wonder this, too.) Like most things in Twitter, there is no Right Answer.

But **there is an average number of tweets per day among all Twitterers,** and it's 4.22. Which is actually a pretty good guide. If you want to build relationships and maintain a positive reputation on Twitter, you should probably post updates at least a few times a week and perhaps a few times a day.

That said, a number of popular Twitterers, including Robert Scoble (@scobleizer) and Guy Kawasaki (@guykawasaki), post dozens of times a day. And researcher Dan Zarrella (@danzarrella) has found that 22 tweets per day is optimal for drawing followers.

The lesson? Start with whatever feels right, and then tweak it to see what works for you.

twitter tip

If you're an average poster, and you occasionally twitter up a storm (say when you're attending a conference, as we discuss in Chapter 4), you should expect some of your followers to be pleased and others to be appalled by the sudden uptick. You can see here that we've drawn a range of reactions for live-twittering events.

[20:43:30] JOHNABYRNE: If you put the video in your most highly trafficked stories and you make sure it's not redundant, you integrate it all. #editorchat

[20:43:39] milehighfool: A tip for tweeps using TweetDeck or another client. You can also filter @colorsign if you prefer. #editorchat

[20:43:42] littlebrownpen: @jimmcbee A lot of the tough questions come from the community. The community holds you accountable to an extent. #editorchat

[20:43:54] ATLCheap: Jennifer Maciejewski, Atlanta-based writer & blogger. Interesting discussion so far; look forward to catching up & jumping in. #editorchat

[20:44:02] wolfemanmatt: RT @JOHNABYRNE We're trying to integrate video with text, placing complementary videos inside stories to change user experience. #editorchat

[20:44:10] JOHNABYRNE: We've been able to quadruple the monthly video streams with this new strategy with no increase in resources & fewer videos. #editorchat

Three cool hashtag tricks

In Chapter 1, we describe hashtags, which let people group messages by category—making them an important element of conversations on Twitter. Once you get the hang of the idea, **you can adapt it for lots of purposes.** Here are a few of our favorite uses:

1. Group chat. Got a discussion you want to hold among a bunch of people who aren't in the same place? Designate a hashtag and a particular hour or so for the chat. Put the word out to the appropriate community. Use a tool like **TweetGrid** (http://tweetgrid.com) or **TweetChat** (http://tweetchat.com) to stay on top of the conversation and moderate it. (Note that hashtags are not case sensitive.)

Here you can see a piece of the transcript for #EditorChat with BusinessWeek.com's editor-in-chief, John Byrne (@JohnAByrne). Although the conversation looks a little disjointed in this format, the forum is emerging as a key place for networking and swapping ideas. For other examples of group chats, check Twitter search for #EventProfs (meeting planners) and #hcmktg (healthcare marketers).

2. Collect ideas. Ask a question on Twitter ("What are your favorite new romance novels?") and give a hashtag people can use to share their answers (#romance09).

3. Share an experience. Loving an American Idol performance? Not so thrilled with Hollywood's latest blockbuster? Just felt a tremble? Use a hashtag to weigh in (#AmericanIdol, #007, #Earthquake). For events like these, in which lots of people participate, there's almost certain to be an existing hashtag. Check Twitter search.

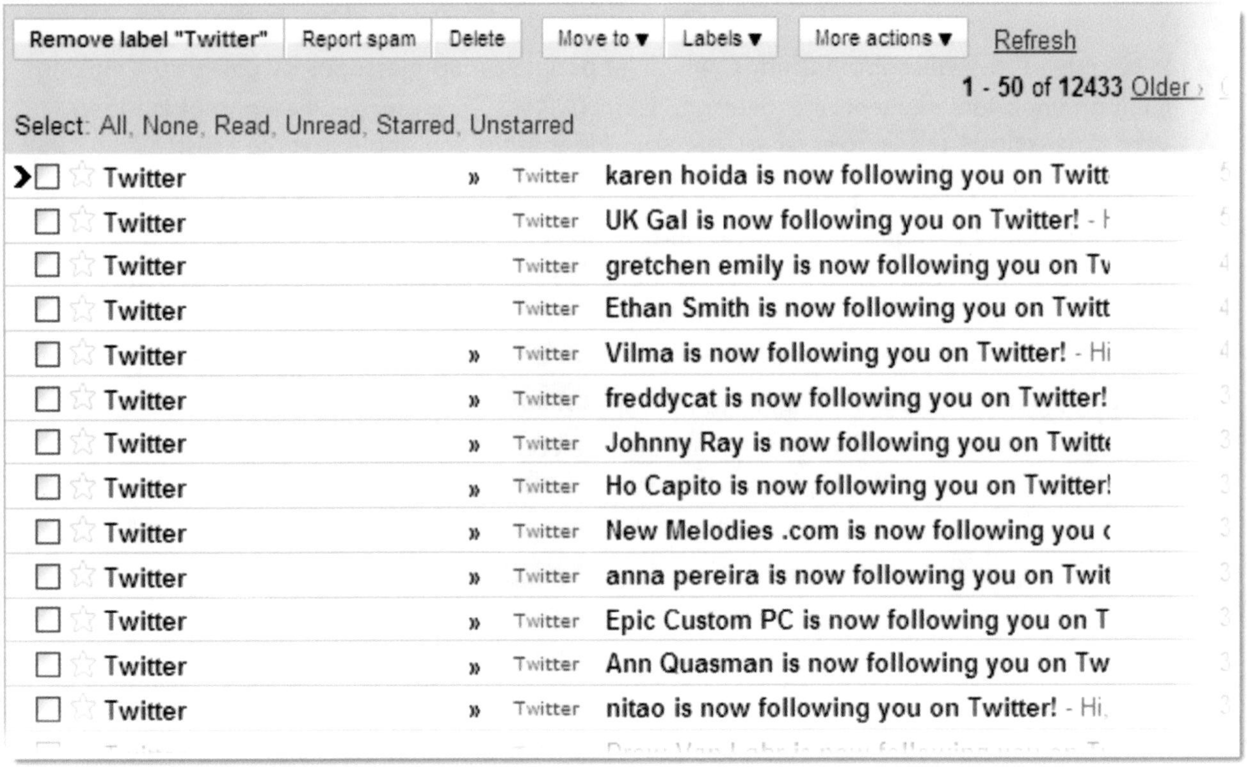
Remove label "Twitter"
Report spam
Delete
Move to
Labels
More actions
Refresh
1 - 50 of 12433 Older ›
Select: All, None, Read, Unread, Starred, Unstarred
Twitter » Twitter karen hoida is now following you on Twitt
Twitter Twitter UK Gal is now following you on Twitter!
Twitter Twitter gretchen emily is now following you on Tv
Twitter Twitter Ethan Smith is now following you on Twitt
Twitter » Twitter Vilma is now following you on Twitter! - Hi
Twitter » Twitter freddycat is now following you on Twitter!
Twitter » Twitter Johnny Ray is now following you on Twitte
Twitter » Twitter Ho Capito is now following you on Twitter!
Twitter » Twitter New Melodies .com is now following you
Twitter » Twitter anna pereira is now following you on Twit
Twitter » Twitter Epic Custom PC is now following you on T
Twitter » Twitter Ann Quasman is now following you on Tw
Twitter » Twitter nitao is now following you on Twitter! - Hi,

Know your new followers

When you first sign up for Twitter, it's set to send you an email every time somebody new follows you. If you don't like the interruption, create an email folder and filter for the messages so that they can pile up without bothering you. Every now and then, you can peek at the list, which will look like the one we've shown here, and **see who you might want to follow back or say hello to.**

Unfortunately, Twitter's notification emails don't contain much info—which means you have to click through if you want to learn about your followers. For richer notices, try **Twimailer** (http://twimailer.com), which will include a follower's profile and most recent tweets. (Twimailer requires that you swap in an email address it gives you, which some people find problematic. Chris Messina [@chrismessina] has a workaround: http://factoryjoe.com/blog/2009/03/04/how-to-use-twimailer-securely.)

twitter tip

If you decide you don't want email notifications from Twitter when you get new followers, you can turn them off under Settings → Notices.

Twittersheep
Search the flock
company making free designer home new things small photographer coach speaker
music way years can entrepreneur real author fun manager
more director now help owner tech creative digital photography technology
services live sales blogger developer guy pr life me lover father love
mom travel expert time here business all work agency art make
working communications writer living good loves products graphic estate too who family one out
marketing
junkie professional advertising traveler online consultant passionate
network news development founder helping our media husband seo
software internet marketer brand dad follow twitter world like
people producer social web design
about us

Three tools to figure out your followers

It doesn't take long to lose track of who's following you and even who you're following. These tools provide **insight into your network.**

1. If you're wondering whether an individual follows you, **DoesFollow** (http://doesfollow.com) will let you check easily.

2. To see all your followees, fans (i.e., followers) and friends (mutual followers), try **FriendOrFollow** (http://friendorfollow.com).

3. If you want to find out what your followers say they're interested in, **Twittersheep** (http://twittersheep.com) will create a tag cloud from the bios of your network. Here you can see the cloud for social media marketing expert Chris Brogan (@chrisbrogan).

twitter tip

If you want to compare followers among two or more accounts, **TweepDiff** (http://tweepdiff.com) described in Chapter 6, can help you out.

twitter

Home   Find People   Help   Sign out   Search

@TweetReport One of my reasons for unfollowing: too many tweets, either unconnected or long-winded serial tweets.

11:13 AM Mar 9th from web in reply to TweetReport

Unfollow graciously

There's no rule saying that once you follow somebody, you have to follow them forever. In fact, one of the useful things about Twitter is that **you can follow somebody for a while, get a sense of their universe, and then unfollow** in order to tune into somebody else for a bit.

Twitter itself doesn't tell somebody when you unfollow her, and in most cases, the person won't know. That said, there are third-party applications that will alert people when they've been unfollowed. Either way, should you tell them why you're unfollowing? Nah. Chances are, you're leaving the account for the very reasons other people love it. (Sarah maintains @TweetReport and received this charmer on a day when several people asked for more twittering.)

To unfollow somebody, head to her account page. Under her picture, click the bar that says "Following," and then in the box that opens, click Remove.

By the way, we can't recommend signing up for unfollow notices yourself. First, they lend to obsessing about popularity. Second, they purport to tell you when people unfollow you after a certain tweet, but they rarely, if ever, show that data accurately. We suggest cultivating good relationships where you can and not worrying about the rest.

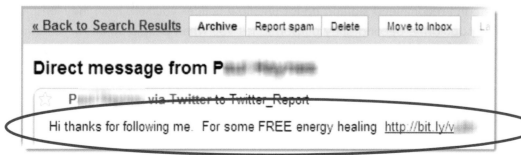

Don't auto-DM (for crying out loud)

Imagine you're at a conference chatting with a few people before the next session starts. Suddenly, somebody shouts across the room, "Nice to meet you! You can learn more about me and my consulting service at www.iampushy.com." From another corner of the room you hear, "Thanks for being in the same room! Can't wait to get to know you!"

You're likely to consider that sort of overture intrusive. And chances are, it's not going to lead to a meaningful exchange.

Auto-DMs—which are generic direct messages some people send when you follow them— work the same way: they're impersonal, disruptive and almost never spark a good conversation. In fact, when you think about them that way, **they sound a lot like spam —which is what they are.**

Take a look at the three examples here: can you imagine the recipient being delighted to get them? (She wasn't.)

If you must acknowledge a new follower, do a little research, figure out what you have in common and send a personal message.

hey guys!!!!!!!! i found a really cool blog which is interesting and helpful,just check it out and just post me ur opinion http://ping ......

5:45 AM Mar 24th from Ping.fm

hey i found a ultra cool blog,check this out,it will help you really,
http:// ████████.blogspot...

1:04 AM Mar 24th from web

@nnphoto Reading My friend ████y's new
blog...http://████████.blogspot... really ultra kool!

12:12 PM Mar 12th from web in reply to nnphoto

@feliciaday Reading My friend ████y's new
blog...http://████████.blogspot... really ultra kool!

12:11 PM Mar 12th from web in reply to feliciaday

@iamdiddy Reading My friend ████y's new
blog...http://████████blogspot... really ultra kool!

12:11 PM Mar 12th from web in reply to iamdiddy

Don't spam anyone

Here's an important point to remember: Twitter is an opt-in medium, which means that **if you're obnoxious or even a little bit spammy, people will unfollow you** or they'll choose not to follow you in the first place. (They can also block you and suggest that you get kicked off Twitter, which we talk about on the next page.) On Twitter, spam is self-defeating.

As we discuss on the last page, auto-DMs are a form of spam. A few other forms of twittering are also spam, and you should avoid all of them.

This ought to go without saying, but if you're DMing people with the goal of selling something, you're committing spam. Don't kid yourself into thinking that a discount or a freebie is a legit message, either. Rule of thumb: if you're tempted to DM a bunch of people you don't know, you're very likely about to become a spammer.

Ditto @messages. If you're sending @messages to people who don't know you, and your notes aren't in response to something they've said or done, or a question or a comment related to their expertise, you'll probably be perceived as a spammer.

Finally, as in email, if your iffy messages contain links, other people are more likely to believe they're spam.

twitter

Samples of spammers: aggressive followers, follow churners, multiple duplicate updates, multiple @ reply spam. Report if you're unsure.

11:11 PM Mar 30th from web

 spam
Spam Watch

136

Fight spam

Internet culture expert Clay Shirky (@cshirky) has said that online social systems are, by definition, "stuff that gets spammed." Twitter is no exception.

Twitter spam comes in two primary forms: random @messages and random direct messages. If you receive an @message from somebody you don't know offering a link to a site that "will make you feel better" or a direct message suggesting that your ultimate happiness is just a click away, you've been spammed. Here's how you can fight it:

Follow Twitter's spam account, http://twitter.com/spam. After they've followed you back (which happens right away), DM them the name of any spammy accounts you encounter. They'll follow up, though they won't send you back a message. (If you need help with a non-spam problem, like a TOS violation or an impersonation, go to http://help.twitter.com and click Submit A Request.) If it's easier for you, you can also send email to spam@twitter.com with details of the spam tweet you received.

Block the spammer. Just head over to the spammer's account page and look on the right side for the Block link. When you block an account, it can no longer send you messages or see yours. In addition, Twitter keeps an eye on blocked accounts to see if they're spam.

Unfollow the spammer. If you're following the account, now's a good time to unfollow it. Go to the spammer's account page, and in the upper-left corner, under the picture, click Following. That opens a box where you can click Remove to unfollow.

CHAPTER 4 | Share Information and Ideas

Twitter is a terrific place to share information and ideas. But with only 140 characters per message—approximately the length of a news headline—clear communication can be challenging.

In this chapter, we look at some of **the smartest ways people have found to post cool information, achieve clarity and make the most of Twitter's space constraint.**

By the way, if you're interested in using Twitter to network and help you find a job, pay special attention to the ideas in this chapter and the next two. Although the last chapter is about business uses of Twitter, a lot of the concepts apply to any professional.

Home Profile Find People Settings Help Sign out

Dubai was designed by a cartoonist who, high on dates and olives, stole porn from the Gods of Air Conditioning and Petroleum.

10:14 PM Apr 6th from web

sacca
Chris Sacca

Home Profile Find People Settings Help Sign out

Isn't junk food part of the "upgrade" on a vacation? Chicago hot dog with all the trimmings, yummm

3:02 PM Apr 3rd from txt

Padmasree

Home Profile Find People Settings Help Sign out

Taking allergy pills is like having Snow White multiple personality disorder. You go from Sneezy/Grumpy to Sleepy/Dopey/Happy.

11:29 AM Apr 9th from web

zappos
Zappos.com CEO -Tony

Be interesting to other people

Twitter routes millions of messages a day about what people are eating for lunch. Not that you shouldn't report on your grilled cheese—or any other details of your day. We're firm believers that exchanging those quotidian snapshots can make people feel more connected to each other.

But do bear in mind that Twitter is an *opt-in* medium. Which means that if you aren't interesting, people will unfollow you or choose not to follow you in the first place.

So before you post a message, take a second to **think about whether there's a more entertaining or informative way to give the update.** Can you make an offbeat observation? Poke a little fun at yourself? Add a link that helps people understand what you're talking about?

Tony Hsieh (@zappos), Chris Sacca (@sacca) and Padmasree Warrior (@Padmasree) are great models: Three big business movers and shakers who talk about business life only by implication, but talk about daily life with great panache.

twitter

Wow, @Bootsy_Collins is twittering. Never occurred to me that could happen.

9:00 PM Apr 29th from twhirl

SarahM
Sarah Milstein

Make sure your messages get seen

Twitter is set to show you only the @messages between people you're following. For example, if you're following Jane but not Joe, you won't see any @messages between Jane and Joe. Conversely, if you're following both Jane and Pete, you'll see the @messages between them.

Hardly anyone is aware of this setting, but it's hugely important. Because it means that when you start a message with the @ symbol, the vast majority of people won't see it. Which may be fine by you if you're sending somebody an @reply, but it's probably the opposite of what you want if you're trying to *refer* to somebody.

For instance, imagine you're followed by 3,500 people, ten of whom are also following Kermit the Frog. When you twitter, "@kermie's new book is amazing; get a copy at http://bit.ly/kerm," only the ten people following both of you will see your message. Which is almost certainly not your intention.

The solution is easy: unless you're sending an @message, don't start your posts with the @ symbol. Instead, rewrite your sentence, or start with something like, "Wow," "Cool," "This just in." You get the idea.

Excellent article from @peterme on the Tropicana carton debacle has a surprise ending. Good lesson here. http://is.gd/kKzI

5:40 PM Feb 24th from twhirl

pahlkadot
Jennifer Pahlka

Funny Video: What if Friendster, MySpace and Facebook shared an apartment http://tinyurl.com/yb29xh ...below Mr Furley

about 4 hours ago from web

jowyang
Jeremiah Owyang

"So what is it that makes some startups successful and leaves others selling off their furniture?" http://bit.ly/A8P3

10:11 AM Mar 20th from web

ericries
Eric Ries

Link to interesting stuff around the Web

Twitter asks, "What are you doing?" But it turns out that the service is also excellent for sharing URLs to the great things you're reading, watching, hearing, cooking and playing.

In addition to **helping other people find cool stuff, there's a self-interested good reason to link liberally:** your messages that contain well-described, cool links are most likely to be retweeted. Plus, if you regularly share great links on a topic, people will come to see you as a resource, which can boost your professional reputation.

From the examples here, you can see that 140 characters is plenty of space to create a *compelling* pointer to a web page and include a shortened URL. (We discuss URL shorteners in Chapters 1 and 6.)

twitter tip

As you can see here, Jennifer Pahlka notes that @peterme (Peter Merholz) is the author of the article she links to. That's a smart idea, not only because it credits him publicly, but also because it lets the author (who may be keeping an eye on his @references) know you like his writing. And that may lead to a new follower.

twitter   Home   Find People   Help   Sign out   Search

i'm taking heat in the comments for this post http://bit.ly/96C91 and some of it well deserved and well said. a much needed discussion

7:29 AM Mar 24th from Power Twitter

fredwilson
Fred Wilson

twitter   Home   Find People   Help   Sign out   Search

Great Wesabe Groups thread on "competing with the Internet" as a local retailer: http://bit.ly/bridalshop

10:23 AM Mar 20th from web

wesabe
Wesabe

twitter   Home   Find People   Help   Sign out   Search

Posted on the Don't Get Caught blog: 5 simple ways PR folk can help/engage bloggers & Twitterers. Add your ideas: http://tinyurl.com/cp4qad

4:36 AM Mar 25th from TweetDeck

dontgetcaught

146

Link appealingly to your blog or site

People and organizations around the Web report that twittering links to their own sites can drive a lot of traffic. Indeed, Twitter has become the top referrer for a lot of sites.

The key to generating click-throughs is writing an appealing little introduction to the post or page you're linking to. Think of it as a headline tailored for your Twitter audience, and—like those we've shown here—consider inviting people to participate.

Do bear in mind that simply posting a feed of headlines from your blog or site can drive people away. Instead, when you post a link, contextualize it for your followers.

Finally, as we mentioned back in Chapter 2, don't forget to leave enough room in your post for people to retweet your message easily.

twitter tip

Want your recent tweets to show up on your blog or site, along with a link to follow you? Twitter has widgets you can use: http://twitter.com/widgets.

I can't drive a motor vehicle on these meds, but no one said anything about glue guns. Or scissors. My hair is a disaster.

10:20 PM Feb 15th from web

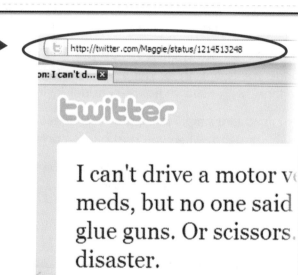

Link to a tweet

Every now and then, you see **a tweet so poignant, smart or funny, you want to send it around** to other people. But how do you link to an individual tweet?

Easy. When you see a message either in your incoming stream of updates or on somebody else's account page, it'll always include the time it was posted. That time stamp is actually a link to the permanent URL for an individual message. Click the time stamp link to open a page with that single message.

A lamb is born! http://snurl.com /ebu04

8:28 AM Mar 22nd from twhirl

dalepd
Dale Dougherty

Home   Find People   Help   Sign out   Search

What 185,000 words looks like: http://www.flickr.com/photo...

2:00 AM Mar 16th from web

doctorow
Cory Doctorow

Home   Find People   Help   Sign out   Search

http://twitpic.com/2a58u - M and I baked muffins this morning. She's getting to be quite the little baker.

10:19 AM Mar 20th from TwitPic

zoefinkel
zoe finkel

Home   Profile   Find People   Settings   Help   Sign out

Post pictures

A picture, as you know, is **worth a good deal more than 140 characters.** Use Twitter to share links to pictures you've posted to on your blog or to photo-sharing sites like Flickr.

To share a picture specifically on Twitter, try a service like **TwitPic** (http://twitpic.com), which lets you post from your phone, the Web and some third-party clients (including those we describe in Chapter 2). The message that shows up on Twitter looks like Zoe Finkel's message here, with a link to the photo on the TwitPic site.

If somebody comments on the TwitPic site, it automatically sends that note as an @reply in Twitter to the original poster. In addition, the site tracks the number of click-throughs to a picture.

twitter tip

Links to pictures, like most other URLs you post to Twitter, really benefit from a snappy little description in your tweet. Which link do you click through, the one that says, "Yesterday in the park" or "Rosie the Rottweiler meets Chico the Chihuahua"?

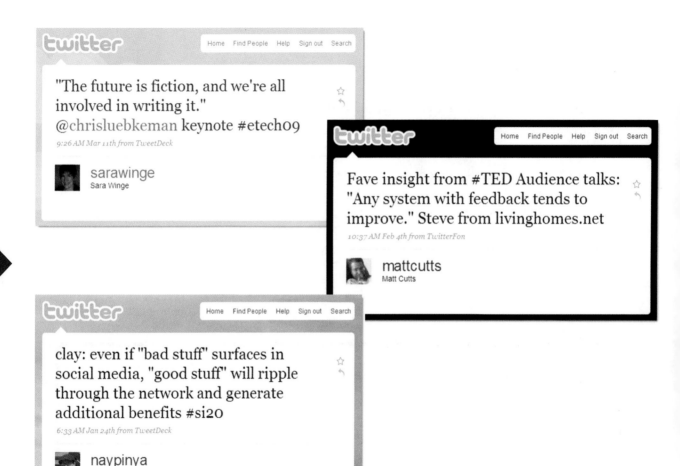

Home   Find People   Help   Sign out   Search

"The future is fiction, and we're all
involved in writing it."
@chrisluebkeman keynote #etech09
9:26 AM Mar 11th from TweetDeck

sarawinge
Sara Winge

Home   Find People   Help   Sign out   Search

Fave insight from #TED Audience talks:
"Any system with feedback tends to
improve." Steve from livinghomes.net
10:37 AM Feb 4th from TwitterFon

mattcutts
Matt Cutts

Home   Find People   Help   Sign out   Search

clay: even if "bad stuff" surfaces in
social media, "good stuff" will ripple
through the network and generate
additional benefits #si20
6:33 AM Jan 24th from TweetDeck

naypinya
Peter Brantley

Live-twitter an event

If you're at a conference or event where people are saying insightful things, Twitter is a **great way to amplify the ideas.** Just type up the juiciest bits and give credit to the speakers. Or share surprising observations. If there's a hashtag for the event, append it.

If you're organizing an event, be sure to encourage live-twittering by creating and publicizing the hashtag. The messages people post will help get the word out about your conference, and if enough people twitter, your event may trend on Twitter search (described in Chapter 2), providing free publicity.

As an organizer, you can take things a step further by projecting tweets from your event on screens around the site or in the meeting rooms. As a speaker, you can designate somebody to track tweets about your talk and give real-time feedback or hold live Q&A via Twitter.

twitter tip

If you're live-twittering an event, put the hashtag at the end of your tweets, not the beginning. Makes them *much* easier for other people to read.

on the austin flight. apparently, sonya needs to "own her job", or those personalized ipods are not going to ship

10:57 AM Mar 13th from web

mala
Danny

OH: "Overall, I'm generally unimpressed with the whole system of human reproduction."

9:21 PM Jan 31st from twitterrific

veen
Jeffrey Veen

OH: "I like going on little errands. Gives me something to Twitter about."

4:48 PM Mar 29th from txt

SarahM
Sarah Milstein

Overhear things

Oddball conversations. One-sided cell phone calls. Funny comments. It's all **good fodder** for the already context-less world of Twitter.

You can just put quotes around the snippets. Or start your message with "Overheard" or "OH" (incidentally, that works for your own thoughts).

2007 SQ6, ~110m-250m in diameter,
just passed the Earth at 10km/s,
missing by ~twenty-five million, eight
hundred thousand km.

about 9 hours ago from Twitter4R

 lowflyingrocks

 CONGRES

No man will ever carry out of the
Presidency the reputation which carried
him into it.

10:01 AM Jan 20th from web

 ThomasJefferson
Thomas Jefferson

Mrs. Hardin here. Mom and Dad went
to Mrs. Johnson's. Took some berry
plants. -April 13, 1937

5:55 AM Apr 13th from web

 Genny_Spencer
Genevieve Spencer

Home   Profile   Find People   Settings   Help   Sign out

Publish on Twitter

By now, you've probably gotten the sense that Twitter is pretty much a blank canvas, waiting for you to fill it with cool stuff. Thing is, that stuff need not be limited to your own bon mots and retweets. In fact, **Twitter can serve very effectively as a publishing platform, letting you share regular posts on a theme.** Just a few of our favorites:

@Genny_Spencer, for a line a day from the 1937 diary of an Illinois farm girl, posted by her great-nephew

@LowFlyingRocks, for announcements of every object that passes close to Earth

@ThomasJefferson, for quotes from the author of the Declaration of Independence (for general quotes, try @IHeartQuotes)

@WordSpy and @emckean, for new words and phrases

twitter tip

Although we generally discourage automated posts for personal and business posting on Twitter, accounts like these are one of the places they can work well. To preschedule messages, try **TweetLater** (http://tweetlater.com). To set up an RSS feed of updates, try **TwitterFeed** (http://twitterfeed.com).

$3,415 raised for Leukemia & Lymphoma Society on Twitter & ONLY 5 HOURS LEFT! (pls RT & donate!) http://bit.ly/t2be #smack09

4:09 PM Mar 26th from web

mashable
Pete Cashmore

Just $44.50 more in @tipjoy @wellwishes pledges in the next 5 minutes and @rosevines will contribute an extra $100 How about it? Please RT?

9:57 AM Dec 19th, 2008 from web

Pistachio
Laura Fitton

Nice to see that @tweetsgiving is almost half way to $10k after just a day on Twitter. Details: http://tweetsgiving.org/ #TweetsGiving

4:42 AM Nov 26th, 2008 from web

jeffpulver
Jeff Keni Pulver

Participate in fundraising campaigns

Fundraising is flourishing on Twitter, most often in micro-form. That is, people organize campaigns in which you're asked to give a very small donation (on another site)—a quarter or a couple of dollars—and perhaps a retweet. When enough Twitterers participate, **the numbers and awareness add up.**

Charity: water (http://www.charitywater.com), for example, has raised several hundred thousand dollars through Twitter-based campaigns and Twestival, a worldwide series of gatherings to benefit the organization.

If you see a campaign roll across your screen, consider participating and passing along the word. Of course, due diligence is always in order: at a minimum, check out the website of the organization sponsoring the event.

If you're looking to organize a campaign on Twitter, sites like **TipJoy** (http://tipjoy.com) can help you with payment processing. Beth Kanter's blog (How Nonprofits Can Use Social Media, http://beth.typepad.com/) can help you figure out what's worked, and what hasn't, in Twitter-based fundraising so far.

A good eye/ear (analytical/emotional) for style, content and nuts&bolts of online communication - @itscomplicated #followfriday

5:49 AM Mar 13th from TweetDeck

deanmeistr
Dean Meyers

Two women w/exceptionally good presentation blogs: @OliviaMitchell @dontgetcaught #followfriday

9:58 AM Mar 20th from twhirl

SarahM
Sarah Milstein

I follow @laureneleonboym for her impeccable taste + diabolical darkly humorous creative output: http://www.boym.com #followfriday

4 minutes ago from TweetDeck

jenbee
Jen Bekman

Make smart suggestions on FollowFriday

To **help each other find cool people to follow,** Twitterers have instituted FollowFriday. The idea couldn't be simpler: on Fridays, you post suggested followers, along with the hashtag #FollowFriday. (Reportedly, Micah Baldwin [@micah] started the trend.)

Trouble is people often post long lists of suggestions (well, as long as you can get in 140 characters) with no explanation. So on Fridays, don't be surprised to see messages scroll by that look like this:

"@cowbell400, @marketingbear, @pineconepeanuts, @superpoke2009, @thatsettlesit, @dubdubdubdc, @halliburton, @seatselectorfriend #FollowFriday"

Seriously, who's going to click through on those? Better to give a little context and list fewer folks. The examples here point you in the right direction.

twitter tip

As we mentioned earlier in this chapter, if you want your post to be seen by most people, don't start it with the @symbol.

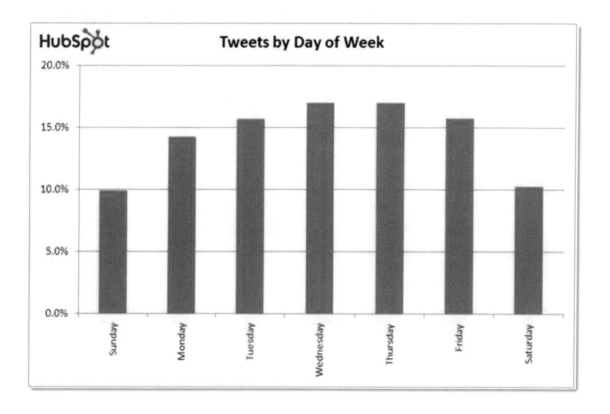

Post on the right days

A number of researchers have found that the most tweets are sent on Tuesdays, Wednesdays and Thursdays. While that may sound like a high-traffic time to avoid, it turns out that's when the most *retweets* are sent, too, suggesting **those are the days when people are most likely to pay attention to your messages.**

Along the same lines, for maximum exposure in the U.S., send your messages during Eastern Time business hours.

The chart here, from HubSpot's late 2008 "State of the Twittersphere" report, shows the mid-week pattern. 2009 research has confirmed the trend. (For the full report, see http://blog.hubspot.com/blog/tabid/6307/bid/4439/State-of-the-Twittersphere-Q4-2008-Report.aspx.)

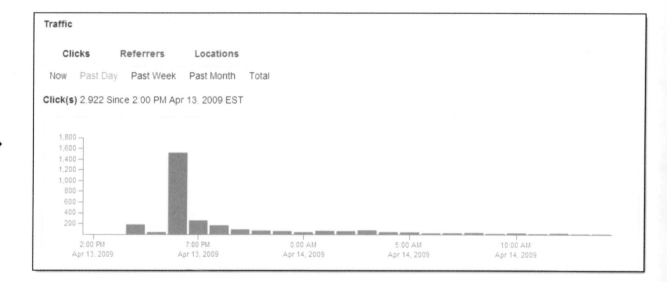

Repost important messages

One of the glorious aspects of Twitter is that, unlike email, it doesn't require a response— or even a glance. Indeed, many people treat it as a river of messages, dipping in when they happen to be next to the stream.

That behavior is important to understand because it means that unless people see your message within five minutes of your posting it, they're very unlikely to see it at all. *Five minutes?* Yup, five minutes. Pete Dimaio (@pdimaio) at Fuel Interactive has done research showing that nearly all responses and retweets happen within five minutes of a posting; after that, responses drop off to nearly nothing. We've seen the same pattern ourselves, and here we've shown it in action: This Bit.ly chart illustrates the click-throughs on a link Tim recently twittered. As you can see, nearly all of the responses occurred right away.

And *that* pattern is important to understand because it means that if you have something important to twitter about, it's a good idea to repeat yourself at least a couple of times, at different hours and probably over the course of several days.

Reposting can feel awkward at first, but you can do it artfully (change your message and refer to the earlier ones), especially if your message is clearly significant, non-commercial and not wildly self-promoting. And bear in mind that each message is just a sentence or two, so you're not imposing much on your followers.

CHAPTER 5 | Reveal Yourself

Twitter asks the question, "What are you doing?" Although people now use Twitter to share the many kinds of ideas and information we describe in Chapter 4, they initially used it to answer that question. So they reported that they were going for a bike ride, making bacon sundaes or watching the dog chew on a sofa cushion. Because they could send updates not only from their computers but from their phones, too, people also twittered that they were sitting next to Bono on a flight to Zimbabwe, being handed a parking ticket on 5th Avenue or getting crummy service at Wal-Mart.

Although status updates like that may sound mundane, people on Twitter have found that **becoming aware of what your friends, family and colleagues are doing leads to a lightweight but meaningful intimacy.** Sociologists refer to this phenomenon as "co-presence," or the sense of being with others. Non-academics, when they have a name for it at all, call it "ambient intimacy" or, more commonly in work situations, "ambient awareness." You could think of it as a cross between ESP and what your mother might call "keeping in touch."

In this chapter, we look at things you can do to boost your personal connections on Twitter.

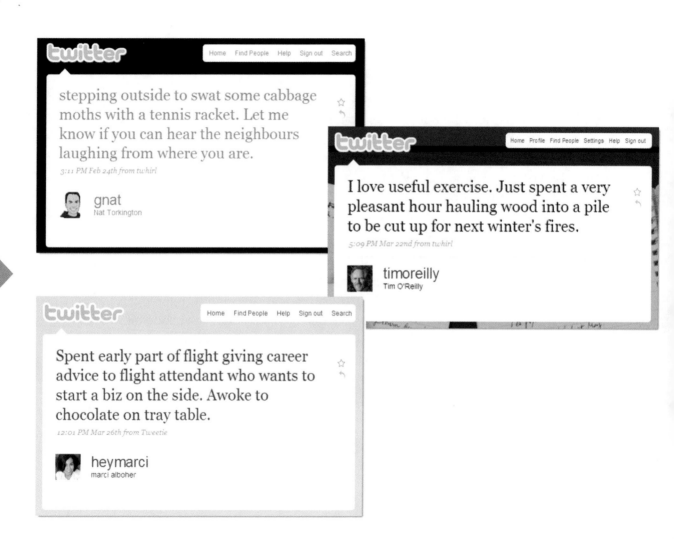

twitter

Home   Find People   Help   Sign out   Search

stepping outside to swat some cabbage
moths with a tennis racket. Let me
know if you can hear the neighbours
laughing from where you are.

3:11 PM Feb 24th from twhirl

gnat
Nat Torkington

twitter

Home   Profile   Find People   Settings   Help   Sign out

I love useful exercise. Just spent a very
pleasant hour hauling wood into a pile
to be cut up for next winter's fires.

5:09 PM Mar 22nd from twhirl

timoreilly
Tim O'Reilly

twitter

Home   Find People   Help   Sign out   Search

Spent early part of flight giving career
advice to flight attendant who wants to
start a biz on the side. Awoke to
chocolate on tray table.

12:01 PM Mar 26th from Tweetie

heymarci
marci alboher

Post personal updates

Whether you use Twitter primarily for professional reasons or personal reasons, **other people like little glimpses into your life**—probably more than you think. It helps them feel connected, it lends authenticity to your voice and it helps you build relationships. As a bonus, it means that when you see each other in person, instead of having a conversation that goes, "How've you been?" "Fine," you can have this conversation:

"Hey, saw that you were in Princeton last week. Did you have a chance to eat at Hoagie Haven?"

"Went twice—once for breakfast. Sounds like you've been busy with your new community garden. I used to have one when I lived in Brooklyn, and I loved it. How's yours going?"

Etcetera.

You don't have to reveal every little detail, but a few small updates can go a long way in fostering friendliness.

Home Profile Find People Settings Help Sign out

Working from a coffee shop in the
Richmond district. If the Richmond was
a car, it would be a gray 1986 Buick
Century.

10:32 AM Jul 16th, 2008 from web

Adam
Adam Rugel

Home Profile Find People Settings Help Sign out

Seeing a baby just makes people happy.
Unless they're boarding a plane.

2:44 PM Mar 3rd from twitterrific

danmil
Dan Milstein

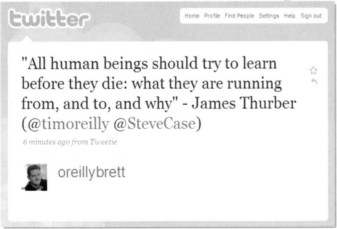

Home Profile Find People Settings Help Sign out

"All human beings should try to learn
before they die: what they are running
from, and to, and why" - James Thurber
(@timoreilly @SteveCase)

6 minutes ago from Tweetie

oreillybrett

Go beyond "What are you doing?"

You don't have to limit your personal posts to answering the question, "What are you doing?" You can **use your 140 characters to post thoughts, observations, advice, funny conversations, poetry, jokes, quotes,** etcetera.

You get the idea. (If you don't, we've included a few choice examples here.)

AA
Ne
Ye

2 m

Tr
op

2 m

Sa
@
dis

2 m

Sk
htt

2 m

bfi
be
#b

2 m

14
stu
Ad

2 m

DV
mo
htt

2 m

lily

2 m

Use the right icon

There are a **couple of things to think about for your icon: fitting in and standing out.**

By "fitting in," we mean: if you want other people to recognize you as a friendly human on Twitter, use a photo or drawing that shows your face recognizably.

By "standing out," we mean: bear in mind that most people will see your Twitter updates while they're glancing at a slew of messages. You can see here that some pop out more clearly than others. Play around with your icon until you hit on a variation that will help people find you in Twitter's small format.

You can find the icon upload under Settings → Picture.

Name Sarah Gila

0
following

0
followers

0
updates

Updates

Name Sarah Gila 🔒
Location Princeton, NJ
Web http://www.linked...
Bio Big on vegetables, dogs, cold weather.

0
following

0
followers

0
updates

Fill out your full bio (it takes two seconds)

When you sign up for Twitter, the system asks you just for your name and username. So it's easy to blow off the rest of your profile settings, which include your location, a URL for you and a brief bio. But **other people like those details,** so jump in and add them.

Bonus: the more information you share, the less you look like a spammer. To wit: which of the accounts shown here are you more likely to follow?

In Chapter 1, we give tips on filling out your profile, which you can find under Settings → Account.

175

Spiff up your background: Part 1

When people click over to your Twitter account page, they get an eyeful. Your icon, your bio, your latest tweets—and your background. The cool thing is that you can customize your background in a number of ways, **bringing some additional personality to your page.**

If you do nothing, your page looks like the upper example here—which isn't bad. If you want to take it another step, you can change just the colors (background, sidebar, links and outlines), as you can see in the middle example. The lower example shows one of several nifty themes Twitter has created for your backgrounding pleasure.

You can take care of all the visual tweaks under Settings → Design.

Spiff up your background: Part 2

To really punch up your Twitter background, upload a photo to create a pleasing wallpaper effect (you can find the option under Settings → Design; any image under 800K works), and then adjust the colors to match, as shown here. Or try a site like **Twitter Gallery** (http://twittergallery.com) for fun themes.

For a custom background that includes more info about you (the Bio field gives you just 160 characters), **TwitBacks** (http://twitbacks.com) offers a bunch of good choices (the PRNewswire profile shown in Chapter 6 uses a TwitBacks template).

You can also **create a fully personalized background** using Photoshop or a similar program. Among the good blog posts on the subject, this one, by Chris Spooner (@chrisspooner), really stands out and includes a flock of good examples: http://www.blog.spoongraphics.co.uk/tutorials/twitter-background-design-how-to-and-best-practices.

If your graphics skill is limited to PowerPoint or Keynote, this post, by Tomas Carrillo (@tomascarrillo), guides you through building a background in your favorite presentation program: http://theclosetentrepreneur.com/create-a-twitter-background-using-powerpoint.

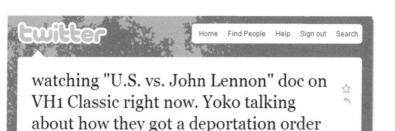

watching "U.S. vs. John Lennon" doc on VH1 Classic right now. Yoko talking about how they got a deportation order under their door in '72.

about 19 hours ago from web

 sreenet
sree sreenivasan

 Sree Sreenivasan watching "U.S. vs. John Lennon" doc on VH1 Classic right now. Yoko talking about how they got a deportation order under their door in '72.

Posted 19 hours ago · Comment · Like

 Tricia Nelson at 6:31pm March 29
I'm watching it too!

 Stanley Mieses at 6:40pm March 29
When the FBI opened its files on Lennon after his death, the photos they kept turned out to be of David Peel, a Lower East Side agit-rocker and acquaintance of Lennon's--but not Lennon!

 Marj Kleinman at 6:56pm March 29
it's a great flick

 George Koshy at 8:05pm March 29
How did you like the movie? I know I watched it a couple of years ago. Don't remember much but I think I found it boring. (And I'm a huge Beatles fan).

 Hina Alam at 12:24am March 30
I love that movie!

Write a comment...

180

Cross-post to your Facebook account

As you have probably noticed, Twitter updates and Facebook status updates are a lot alike. The biggest difference is that on Twitter, your messages are probably public, whereas on Facebook, only people you've mutually approved can see what you're up to.

Given the similarity, it may make sense to cross-post and **have messages you send out on Twitter also show up on Facebook.** There are two common reasons you might cross-post:

1. You tend to be inactive on Facebook, so feeding in tweets livens up your Facebook presence.

2. You use Facebook to connect with a lot of casual acquaintances, and feeding in tweets lets you collect a lot of comments.

Many third-party programs will let you cross-post automatically (see Chapter 2 for a few recommendations). You can also use a Facebook app to help you out. **Selective Twitter Status** (http://apps.facebook.com/selectivetwitter/) lets you choose which tweets also post to Facebook. **The Twitter Facebook app** (http://apps.facebook.com/twitter/) cross-posts all of your tweets. To post simultaneously across a bunch of social networking sites, try **Ping.fm** (http://ping.fm).

bonniedone

▼ ✓ Following ✓ Device updates ON

You follow bonniedone   Remove

bonniedone's updates appear in your timeline.

Device updates

● On   ○ Off

You will receive bonniedone's updates via SMS.

Keep track of friends and family

If you find that following a flock of professional contacts and celebrities means you forget to connect with friends and family on Twitter, **use a tool that helps you see their messages easily.**

Three ideas:

1. Grab the RSS feeds for your high-priority accounts (described in Chapter 1).

2. Get phone updates just for the people whose messages you want to be certain you see (shown here and described in Chapter 1).

3. Use TweetDeck (described in Chapter 3) or another third-party app that lets you group incoming messages.

CHAPTER 6 | Twitter for Business: Special Considerations and Ideas

If you're twittering on behalf of your company or in a primarily professional capacity, you've got a few additional challenges to make your Twitter account successful. In fact, everything we've said already applies to you; here we discuss **additional considerations and ideas to make your company's twittering really sing.**

If you want examples of other companies on Twitter, check out **TrackingTwitter** (http://trackingtwitter.com), which lists brands, media, television and celebrities. **Twibs** (http://twibs.com), another directory, isn't limited to brands. **ExecTweets** (http://exectweets.com) showcases the twittering of businesspeople.

Incidentally, if you're interested in *internal* micromessaging for your organization—which a lot of companies find to be an inbox-freeing revelation—two of the top providers are **Yammer** (http://yammer.com) and **Present.ly** (http://presentlyapp.com).

 | Verizon | Search

Realtime results for Verizon

0.04 seconds

 SemanticBot: #SemanticBlogs : Tech News: **Verizon** Wireless Hub | Jaguwar's Musings http://tinyurl.com/ckxnjf (expand)

2 minutes ago from *twitterfeed* · Reply · View Tweet

 batackett: **Verizon** needs to trian it's employees how to set up the HUB, this is rediculous!

2 minutes ago from *Tweetie* · Reply · View Tweet

 marioferguson: **Verizon**'s VZNavigator just got me lost for Fry's Electronic. I had to in old school and get directions by calling the store, haha.

5 minutes ago from *Ping.fm* · Reply · View Tweet

 charlesmunro: What a great day outside! Sadly, my cell phone locked up (3rd time) so I'm spending part of my Saturday standing in line at **Verizon**.

11 minutes ago from *web* · Reply · View Tweet

Listen first

The **biggest mistake we see companies make when they first hit Twitter** is to think about it as a channel to push out information. In fact, it turns out to be a great medium for holding *conversations* rather than for making announcements.

People already on Twitter will expect your corporate account(s) to engage with them, so before you start twittering away, spend a few weeks or so understanding the ways people talk about you. Get a sense for the rhythms of conversation on Twitter, and think about how you'll hold conversations.

No matter your sector, chances are that people are already twittering about your products, your brand, your company or at least your industry. In Chapter 2, we cover a range of listening tools and techniques; later in this chapter, we address a few more.

twitter tip

Some companies and consultants build customer relationships by keeping an eye on Twitter search for questions they can answer, and then carefully approaching the person who's asked the question. If you use this method, be sensitive to the fact that people might not want to hear from you.

What will be different in three months, six months or a year **because we've engaged on Twitter?**

Have clear goals

Because it's so lightweight, Twitter may tempt you to just dive in and give it a try. Which is a reasonable approach if you're an individual.

But **for companies, an unfocused stab at twittering can lead to accounts that don't represent the business well or that conflict with other communication channels.** Twitter is littered with corporate accounts that somebody started with good intentions but then abandoned after a short period, leaving a permanent, public record of corporate neglect. In addition, twittering can suck up staff time; why assign resources to Twitter if you don't know what you're hoping to get out of it?

Twitter gives you an unparalleled opportunity to build relationships with customers and other constituents, and we suggest you think of it in those terms, rather than as part of a campaign. That said, you can do yourself a big favor by spending some time thinking through what you'd most like to get out of your account or accounts and whether you'll measure that.

Your goals might include things like: better serving your existing customers; increasing your customer base; offering customer service; connecting with potential partners; and so forth.

What are your cooking habits (or lack thereof)? Check out our survey via Facebook (see right column) http://is.gd/j4h6

12:38 PM Feb 26th from TweetDeck

 WholeFoods
Whole Foods Market

twitter

@penneyv Best thing to do would be to contact Customer Service of the Charleston store directly: 843.971.7240.

11:48 AM Jan 30th from TweetDeck

 WholeFoods
Whole Foods Market

Integrate with your other channels

Twitter is cool, but it's not magic. It's part of your communications toolkit, and it probably fits with at least a few of your departments or functions: customer service, PR, marketing, product development, human resources, etcetera—all of whom are using a bunch of tools to connect with people.

For instance, if you think of your account as an information booth where you share tips, links, promos and so forth, but people come to you with questions and complaints, your company needs to be able to respond with appropriate information. We've too often seen corporate accounts that post messages like, "@customer: That's a shame. Call us to get the problem resolved." And then there's no phone number given. For a customer who's already having a problem, that sort of reply simply amps up her frustration. Much better to provide specific contact info, or even take the conversation to DM, get the customer's contact info, and then have customer service follow up.

To have accounts that truly engage on behalf of your company, make sure people throughout your organization are aware of any corporate twittering and that you have some basic systems set up to route and resolve inquiries and complaints. Of course, if you spend time listening, as we recommend earlier in this chapter, you'll be able to plan ahead for the kinds of queries you might need to field.

In addition to integrating with your departments, coordinate your Twitter, Facebook and other social media accounts to provide consistent information.

192

TweetStats
Makin' Your Graf!

Tweet Stats   Tweet Cloud

TweetStats for marscafe (Tweet This!)
Last updated 11 Apr 2009 at 12:54

Your Tweet Timeline - 4.7 tweets per day (tpd)

Start slow, then build

A big concern execs—and pretty much everyone—has about Twitter is that it will be **a black hole of time for employees.** And it can be.

To avoid that problem altogether, start slow, posting perhaps once a day or just a few times a week and answering questions several times a day. Then, if the account proves useful, start devoting more time and resources to it. If it doesn't pan out, you haven't put a hard-to-justify amount of time into it.

Here we use **TweetStats** (http://tweetstats.com) to look at the Twitter activity for Des Moines' Mars Café. They started off slow, found Twitter to be a useful tool, and then amped up their posting. (The last month is low because at the time of this screenshot, the month had just started.)

Hi! I'm Tony Hsieh the CEO of Zappos.com.

Have a question? Here's how to get the fastest response:

Customer service:
Help finding a product
cs@zappos.com
1-800-927-7671

Interviews, PR:
Speaking requests
pr@zappos.com

Marketing, Sponsorships
Donation & Charity Requests:
solicitation@zappos.com

Merchandising:
Steve Hill, VP Merchandising
shill@zappos.com

Job Inquiries:
http://jobs.zappos.com

Inside Zappos:
http://blogs.zappos.com

zappos

▸ ✓ Following   – Device updates OFF

http://twitpic.com/3a6nl - Enjoyed touring Etsy.com offices & meeting w/ CEO. Met a nice giant owl too.

about 20 hours ago from TwitPic

I don't like the phrase "social media" b/c the default assumption w/ "media" is that the publisher is the main benificiary.
9:15 PM Apr 12th from txt

At dinner w/ @chafkin who told me his actress girlfriend is just starting to meet Asians. I felt special, then realized he said "agents".
6:31 PM Apr 11th from txt

http://twitpic.com/347hr - Gotta love NY. Dog trying to make Puss-In-Boots jealous. Wonder if it's heard of Zappos?
1:01 PM Apr 10th from TwitPic

At airport about to fly to NY. FYI a redeye reduction camera does not actually reduce the number of redeye flights one takes.
11:07 PM Apr 9th from txt

Na
Lo
W
Bi
bl
tw

3
fr

Ur

Fr

A
m
nu
b

Fr

Figure out who does the twittering

Twitter is a social medium. So **if you have to choose between a person who has perfect information to share but doesn't really get or like twittering and a person who totally embraces the medium,** choose the latter. Then find a way to support that person with extra information and access to the people who tend to be your knowledge hubs.

Incidentally, we can't recommend outsourcing your twittering to a PR, ad or marketing agency. While that might appear to be an appealing time-saver, it's highly unlikely to yield the kinds of relationships that customers expect, and it could easily backfire if people get the feeling they're being sold to.

In fact, some of the most successful Twitterers are also the busiest. Check out **ExecTweets** (http://exectweets.com) for a list of C-level businesspeople who twitter. Some executive Twitterers (like @timoreilly or @JohnAByrne) share the information flow of their business; others, like @zappos, mostly share the flow of their lives. But it doesn't have to be an either/or deal: check out how effectively Tony Hsieh promotes Zappos on his Twitter page!

twitter

Home   Find People   Help   Sign out   Trends ▼   Search now   🔍

prnewswire

Follow

@helenmosher He looks much to old to be your son! Mine is on Twt too and sometimes @s me or RTs me. We giggle about it ;)

about 10 hours ago from TweetDeck in reply to helenmosher

@ProfNet A lot of interesting people, talking about a lot of interesting things on Twt!
about 11 hours ago from TweetDeck in reply to ProfNet

@gethr0 If you are a content creator (blogger, journalist, analyst, etc), you can sign up for PRNJ www.prnewswire.com/media/
about 11 hours ago from TweetDeck in reply to gethro

Some days you are the tweeter, some days you are the retweeter, but today I am mostly the tweader... I mean reader

PR Newswire

Victoria Harres Akers

✉ victoria.harres
@prnewswire.com

Vicky is the Director of Audience Development at PR Newswire. She was born in Brazil, lives in Texas, loves to cook for her friends and family, and is always fascinated by anything techie...including people!

Website:
prnewswire.com/

Name PR Newswire
Location Global
Web http://www.prnews...
Bio I'm Vicky, PR Newswire's Director of Audience Development. I love to chat about the who-what-when-where of media/social media.

8,047	9,446	2,592
following	followers	updates

Updates

Favorites

Actions
block prnewswire

Following

Reveal the person behind the curtain

The **biggest opportunity Twitter gives you is the chance to show the personality and humanness behind your organization.** When you do so, you create the Petri dish in which you can grow conversations with people and establish relationships on a relatively intimate level.

But people aren't interested in connecting with a nameless, faceless entity. So once you've decided who's going to do the twittering for your company, be absolutely sure to identify him or her on your Twitter account page.

In your profile settings (under Settings → Account), use the Name field to identify the company, and then use the 160-character Bio to identify the person or people behind the account.

The right-side bio for this PR Newswire account says, "I'm Vicky, PR Newswire's Director of Audience Development. I love to chat about the who-what-when-where of media/social media." Then she's filled out the rest of the profile nicely and taken identification a beautiful step further by creating a custom background (described in Chapter 5) that includes her picture, email address and a more detailed bio.

When people connect with this account, they really know who they're getting.

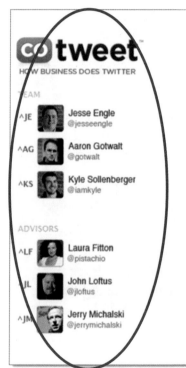

co tweet

HOW BUSINESS DOES TWITTER

TEAM

^JE — Jesse Engle @jesseengle

^AG — Aaron Gotwalt @gotwalt

^KS — Kyle Sollenberger @iamkyle

ADVISORS

^LF — Laura Fitton @pistachio

JL — John Loftus @jloftus

^JM — Jerry Michalski @jerrymichalski

twitter

Home   Find People   Help   Sign out   Trends

    cotweet

Follow

@armintalic Dude, you rock! Thanks so much for the feedback. Taking it all in now. Looks like you've been reading our minds a bit! ^KS

about 14 hours ago from CoTweet

@armintalic Looking forward to seeing your ideas. Love this kind of feedback. Thanks! ^KS

about 17 hours ago from CoTweet in reply to armintalic

Name
Web
Bio Co
Does

4,03
follow

Upda

Favor

Action
bloc

Follo

Manage multiple staff Twitterers

If you've got more than one person twittering from an account, **you need a way to identify the crew.** It's a good idea to have a three-pronged approach:

1. Include names in the 160-character Bio. That's the place that search engines look for information, and it's also the place the Twitter API will draw from to represent your account in third-party clients and applications (described in Chapter 2). Of course, 160 characters isn't much room, and you may wind up just listing first names and perhaps the team department.

2. Create a custom background, like the one shown here, to identify everyone. The vast majority of people will see your account on the Twitter website, and a custom background like this—which includes the name, picture, personal accounts and initials for each person—is a great way to go.

3. Sign messages with the initials of whomever is posting. Just prefix the initials with a piece of punctuation to help signal that it's a signature.

Dell on Twitter : Follow Us

Dell Offers, News, Blogs, & Community Sites on Twitter

Perhaps you already use Twitter to communicate with your friends, find out about breaking news, and keep up with technology and social media (or even political) leaders.

Now you can also get great deals from Dell, stay current with what's happening at Dell, and connect with other Dell fans and employees through Twitter!

Dell Offers on Twitter

DellOutlet
Exclusive Twitter discounts and news directly from the Dell Outlet.
▸ Go to DellOutlet Twitter
▸ Managed by: StefanieatDell

DellOutletIE
IRELAND Refurbished Dell™ computers & electronics with with the same standard limited warranties as we do on our new systems.
▸ Go to DellOutlet Ireland Twitter
▸ Managed by: StephenjatDell

DellOutletUK
UK Refurbished Dell™ computers & electronics with with the same standard limited warranties as we do on our new systems.
▸ Go to DellOutlet UK Twitter
▸ Managed by: StephenjatDell

DellHomeOffers

Dell/Alienware News on Twitter

Direct2Dell
Headlines from our blog about Dell products, services, and customers.
▸ Go to Direct2Dell Twitter
▸ Written by: LionelatDell

Alienware
Offering High-performance gaming PCs news, products and updates from Alienware.
Go to Alienware Twitter ⬅

Dell English Blogs on Twitter

DellYourBlog
Headlines from our blog -- Dell Digital Life : Your Blog.
▸ Go to DellYourBlog Twitter
▸ Lead Editor/Moderator: JohnatDell

DellChannel
Headlines from the blog -- A voice of PartnerDirect.
▸ Go to DellChannel Twitter
▸ Written by: APaxtonatDell

Coordinate multiple accounts

It's one thing to have multiple people twittering from the same organizational account, but what if you've got several corporate accounts? **Identify your array of accounts in two obvious places** to help people understand which ones will be of interest to them:

1. Create a page on your website that lists all the accounts. As you can see here, Dell—which has dozens of Twitter accounts—has grouped them, and then listed the icon and a description for each account; it's also linked not only to the described account but to the personal account of the person who maintains it.

2. In your custom background, list other relevant Twitter accounts. For example, if you have a few customer service accounts, show all of those. For a good illustration, see http://twitter.com/comcastcares.

twitter tip

To help people find and understand your various accounts, have them talk to each other. They can retweet one another, refer to each other, and exchange messages. No need to overdo it, but don't avoid interaction either.

twitter

 kodakCB

▸ ✓ Following

Kodak's

Name Kodak Chief Blogger
Location Rochester, NY
Web http://jennycisne...
Bio Jennifer Cisney - Kodak's
Chief Blogger. Design Geek.
Photography Nut. Check out
kodak.com/go/followus

2,065	2,132	1,212
following	followers	updates

Name Kodak Chief Blogger
Location Rochester, NY
Web http://jennycisne...
Bio Jennifer Cisney - Kodak's
Chief Blogger. Design Geek.
Photography Nut. Check out
kodak.com/go/followus

2,065	2,132	1,212
following	followers	updates

Updates

Favorites

Make sure you're findable

A **common mistake organizations make on Twitter is filling out the profile in a way that makes it hard for people to find your company** when they search for you (under Find People → Find on Twitter).

The problem arises when you use the Name field to list the person who does the twittering. Instead, put the company name there, and describe the person in the Bio field. Why? Because Twitter's search looks in the Name field, not the Bio to determine whether the account somebody is searching for exists. And in the vast majority of cases, people search for your company name, not your employee's name.

In addition, the Name rather than the username is what Twitter uses when it emails somebody to say you've followed her. So if your account name is GeneralElectric, but your Name is Joe Smith, people will get notifications that Joe Smith is following them, and they may not realize the account is really for GE.

H hoovers

▸ ✓ Following

"Smart marketers think in terms of their audience's plain English, not their own." @rsomers brings wisdom: http://is.gd/r1Yj

11 minutes ago from TweetDeck

@unmarketing Wow, I didn't know Hortons *made* anything that could take 11 minutes.

about 1 hour ago from TweetDeck in reply to unmarketing

@SheilaS I like your "spray-n-pray" formulation. How effective are those p.r. e-mails? Ever?

about 1 hour ago from TweetDeck in reply to SheilaS

@ScottHepburn I'm with you all the way: "use" is infinitely superior to "utilize." Ditto "now" or "yet" for "at this point in time."

about 1 hour ago from TweetDeck in reply to ScottHepburn

Updates

Favorites

Actions

message hoovers
hoovers

Following

Be conversational

As we discuss earlier in this chapter, Twitter is a terrific medium for conversation, and it's what people on the system expect. In fact, if you refrained from one-way PR blasts and instead participated in lots of exchanges, you'd be **using Twitter in a way that you can't do with any other communication channels.**

What does conversation look like? A lot of @messages, as described in Chapters 1 and 3. This Hoovers account is a good example: three of the four messages you can see are @replies, and the top message uses the @ convention to refer to the author of the article listed. Increasingly, corporate and organizational accounts look like this.

(Remember: @replies are usually seen only by people following both parties to the conversation. So if you want your reply to be seen by all your followers, don't put the @ at the very beginning of the tweet. For more on this important issue, see Chapter 4.)

twitter   Home   Find People   Help   Sign out   Search

RT @danbarham: Found this cool old
projector while clearing out the office...
It still works! http://twitpic.com/2mdta
- Cool!

about 8 hours ago from TweetDeck

kodakCB
Kodak Chief Blogger

twitter   Home   Find People   Help   Sign out   Search

RT @Spotts016: @jetblue suggestions
for what to do at night in D.C.? - I don't
but maybe the Twitter crowd does
#TTIAD

7:38 AM Mar 26th from TweetDeck

JetBlue
JetBlue Airways

Retweet your customers

As we discuss in Chapters 1 and 3, retweeting is an essential part of the way people hold conversations on Twitter. **To really be part of the community,** then, do as the Romans do and retweet people.

Doing so shows them respect and amplifies their voices—both great actions for building relationships. It also shows that you have similar interests (as in the Kodak example here), or that you're happy to help get their question answered (as in the JetBlue example).

2

crowdvine: @karenblakeman Sorry to hear that. Is there something specific we can help you with (or possibly even add)?

4 days ago · Reply · View Tweet

karenblakeman: @bucchere Thanks for the pointer but have no choice but to use **crowdvine**. Conference organisers want all their speakers to use it

4 days ago · Reply · View Tweet · 💬 Show Conversation

bucchere: @karenblakeman Frustrated with **Crowdvine**? Check out http://www.thesocialcollective.com

4 days ago · Reply · View Tweet · 💬 Show Conversation

interaction09: Also, join the **crowdvine** network for the conference at: http://interaction09.**crowdvine**.com/

5 days ago · Reply · View Tweet

chainreaction: Reminder to join our networking site for people to 'meet' each other before the #chainreaction event http://chain-reaction.**crowdvine**.com/

5 days ago · Reply · View Tweet

1

karenblakeman: Not getting far with **crowdvine**. Even less intuitive than Facebook!

5 days ago · Reply · View Tweet

Offer solid customer support

As we discuss earlier in this chapter, whether you set up your account with customer service in mind, you'll likely get such inquiries. The cool thing about Twitter is that **you can reply in public,** demonstrating your company's responsiveness. Even better, if one person asks a question, it's likely a bunch of people have the same issue, so answering publicly can help a lot of folks at once. (Of course, some inquiries are specialized; take those to DM.)

In addition to direct questions you get, you can keep an eye on Twitter search (see Chapter 2) and respond to complaints about your company, as shown here. If you approach people like this, do so gently; some will be pleased to hear from you, others may find it a bit creepy.

If your company has a very high volume of customer service messages, consider opening an account or several just for customer service. @ComcastCares is the gold standard for this model.

twitter tip

Earlier in this chapter, we talk about the importance of making sure that the person or people running your Twitter account are integrated with your customer service arm. Otherwise, you can easily create more steps for customers who are trying to resolve problems.

twitter   Home   Find People   Help   Sign out   Search

Cool! iPhone app for finding free ATMs near you: http://tinyurl.com/ac53co

5:00 PM Mar 4th from web

☆
↩

wesabe
Wesabe

twitter   Home   Find People   Help   Sign out   Search

"Someone is storing his Richard Serra sculptures along the East River in the Bronx" - http://tr.im/ecoq (via greg.org)

6:38 AM Feb 3rd from TweetDeck

☆
↩

MuseumModernArt
Museum of Modern Art

Post mostly NOT about your company

Kathy Sierra has said, "With few exceptions, the worst mistake a 'business blog' can make is to blog about the business." The same principle holds true in Twitter.

If you're a brand that a lot of people already adore, you can probably get away with posting mostly about your own company—people love you, and they want more. But if you're an unknown entity to most people, or if you have a mixed reputation, or if you just want to take your Twitter relationships to another level, **think about Twitter as a way to exchange mutually interesting information.**

So rather than post a lot of information about your company, aim instead to post mostly third-party links, resources and tips that would be of interest to people who follow you. The examples shown here both do exactly that.

Wesabe is a personal finance site, and they're all about cool ways to save money; the link shown here goes to another site that describes an iPhone app for finding free ATMs. In the Museum of Modern Art example, the link is to a blog that has no affiliation with MoMA, but the story about sculptor Richard Serra is of great interest to his fans. MoMA counts itself among that group, and a lot of its followers are likely to do so, too.

Taking this approach helps build your credibility with customers, potential customers and other constituents. It also makes you a more likely go-to source for journalists.

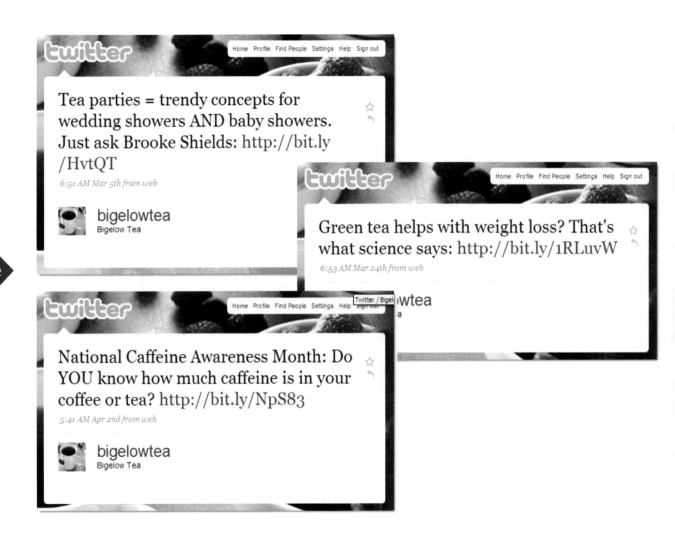

Link creatively to your own sites

Even if you use Twitter primarily to post information that's not directly about your company, you can—and should—use it to sometimes link back to your own site or blog. Many companies find that Twitter can become a top referrer to their sites, so avail yourself of that benefit—just do it in a smart way.

The key is to frame the link in a way that's interesting to your Twitter followers. So instead of saying, "New Blog Post: Mundane Headline, http://yourblog.com," try something like the examples here, each of which links back to the Bigelow Tea blog.

twitter tip

If you're looking to get the most out of Twitter, don't fall into the trap of posting an RSS feed of headlines from your site or blog. Although there are services that will automate such a connection for you, they simply help you create an impersonal account that duplicates the main feature of an RSS reader. Why bother?

Awesome price - Dell Outlet Studio™
Hybrid desktop PCs starting at $399 -
http://is.gd/oLYD

1:44 PM Mar 24th from web

DellOutlet
Dell Outlet

pls retweet: @namecheap is offering
free domains in their next trivia contest
tomorrow as well as 3 dell mini
netbooks! http://is.gd/9xMw

9:12 AM Mar 9th from twhirl

NameCheap
NameCheap.com

Don't forget our Exclusive Twitter deal:
save an additional 30% on a Swing-arm
Plug-in Bronze Lamp with Oatmeal
Shade http://bit.ly/4jJBYx

3:02 PM Apr 9th from Power Twitter

Overstock
Overstock.com

Make money with Twitter

Because Twitter can drive a lot of traffic to your sites (as we mentioned on the previous page), think hard about how you can **use it to help people find good deals you offer.** Among the successful tactics companies use:

1. Promotions. Offer Twitter-specific discount codes. Some companies report that lower-priced items are much more likely to get uptake. Do some testing to see what works for you.

2. Contests. If there's one thing the Twitterverse loves, it's a good contest. Fun, creative games with good rewards can generate a lot of attention. (If you run a contest, be sure to describe it on your website and include legal details.)

3. Sale announcements. Let people know when you run a great sale. Or if you run an outlet, post choice new items as they hit your inventory.

By the way, contests and solid deals tend to get retweeted, so they can be a good way of drawing not just business, but legitimate new followers, too. Also, if you offer deals, try posting them a number of times to get on the radar of a lot of people.

twitter

The site is having some hiccups - we're fixing it and hope to have the problems resolved shortly. We'll tweet when all is well.

3:55 PM Mar 19th from TweetDeck

 hulu

twitter

Everything should be back to normal now. Thanks for your patience!

4:26 PM Mar 19th from TweetDeck

 hulu

Report problems...and resolutions

Twitter is a great place to acknowledge that your company is having some kind of problem. Your site is down. Your conference hotel ballroom is flooded. One of your stores has run out of Cabbage Patch Kids. **Letting people know that you're aware of the issue— and that it may be causing them some pain—is just good, human service.**

Of course, Twitter also gives you the chance to let people know you've rectified the situation.

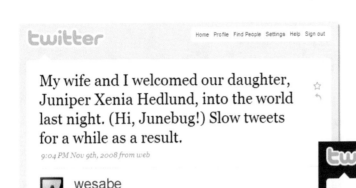

Twitter

Home Profile Find People Settings Help Sign out

My wife and I welcomed our daughter, Juniper Xenia Hedlund, into the world last night. (Hi, Junebug!) Slow tweets for a while as a result.

9:04 PM Nov 9th, 2008 from web

wesabe
Wesabe

Twitter

Home Profile Find People Settings Help Sign out

We're watching Speidi on The View right now, is anyone else?

8:50 AM Mar 13th from web

TVGuide
TV Guide

Twitter

Home Find People Help Sign out Search

http://twitpic.com/1bf2e - Folks starting to abandon Mothership... don't think the heavy stuff's gonna come down for quite a while.

1:23 PM Feb 3rd from TwitPic

DunkinDonuts
Dunkin' Donuts

Post personal updates

As we said earlier in this chapter, **Twitter gives you a phenomenal chance to reveal the human side of your organization,** helping people connect with a person or people who work for you. That starts with identifying your Twitterers. The next step is posting the occasional personal update.

The personal updates don't have to be constant, and it's fine if they're work-related. But do add them in sometimes, as your followers like getting them a lot more than you probably expect.

For instance, the Dunkin Donuts post here is a link to the company's HQ parking lot during a snowstorm. Sound mundane? 400 people have clicked through to check it out.

You might be surprised, but little posts like that can go a long way toward building relationships.

bit.ly
Shorten, share, and track your links

Welcome, sgmils. Account | Sign out

Home | Tools | Search | Blog

Info ⊕

Title:

Long Link:

bit.ly Link:

Traffic:

Locations:

Conversations:

Google Maps

http://maps.google.com/maps?f=d&saddr=New+York+Penn+Station&
daddr=9th+Ave+%26+14th+St.+New+York,+NY&hl=en&geocode=&mra=ls&
dirflg=r&date=11%2F12%2F08&time=4:13pm&ttype=dep&noexp=0&noal=0&
sort=&sll=40.746175,-73.998395&sspn=0.014468,0.036392&ie=UTF8&z=14

http://bit.ly/CUjV ⊕

1,716 Click(s) View All

United States 827; United Kingdom 56; Germany 52 View All

Twitter 0; FriendFeed 0; Comments on Page 0 View All

Share   Copy

220

Use URL shorteners to track click-throughs

Using Twitter to help drive traffic to your sites? Measuring that traffic is a smart thing to do. If you have Google Analytics or a similar measuring package, you're all set. But if you don't have access to those tools or the wherewithal to get them set up, **a URL shortener that tracks click-throughs is a quick and dirty way to gauge traffic.**

Among the services that track: **Bit.ly** (http://bit.ly); **Tr.im** (http://tr.im); and **Cli.gs** (http://cli.gs). (They all let you create custom short URLs, too.)

Tracking through URL shorteners is an imperfect system because some people will change the original URL when they retweet you. Still, using a shortener can give you a sense of the traffic you're gaining from Twitter. For an extra measure of measurement, try **TweetReach** (http://tweetreach.com), which shows how many people may have seen a post.

twitter tip

For a mind-blowingly thorough discussion and review of URL shorteners, see Danny Sullivan's (@dannysullivan) article, "URL Shorteners: Which Shortening Service Should You Use?" (http://searchengineland.com/analysis-which-url-shortening-service-should-you-use-17204).

twitter

skydiver

Follow

Peter Shankman

Social Media CEO Adventurist.

Likes cats. Hates Jell-O.

Biz travels way too much.

www.shankman.com

222

UrgHARO: randee@gmail.com at Fox Nws needs celeb agents to tlk abt $$ freed ship captain can make on movie rightrs/story - HARO in subject

about 4 hours ago from TwitterBerry

Called it yesterday on whoh.com that there'd be front page stories about the first dog. See USAT this morning. See? U should read whoh.com!

about 4 hours ago from TwitterBerry

East bound and down... Loaded up and truckin', we're gonna do what they say can't be done...

about 19 hours ago from TwitterBerry

UrgHARO: NYC-area moms over 55 who keep in touch with their kids on Facebook. Email Helpareporter@gmail.com & put HARO-FACEBOOK MOMS sub?

Name Peter Shankman
Location New York
Web http://www.shankm...
Bio Social Media CEO Adventurist, founder of Help A Reporter Out (HARO) - http://tinyurl.com/6odo4k

728	36,492	3,820
following	followers	updates

Updates

Favorites

Actions
block skydiver

Following

Engage journalists and PR people

Twitter is home to thousands of journalists, media workers and PR people. If you're looking to get a little exposure for your company, **Twitter can be a great place to connect with these folks.** Here are a few tips for doing so:

1. Post great messages. If your Twitter account is a resource in your sector, journalists will trust you quite a bit more. And they may even find you through RTs and comments other people make.

2. Follow the media people who cover your sector. Often, they twitter out when they're looking for sources. In addition, following them is a step toward building a relationship—but proceed with caution; they have a lot of people trying to buddy up to them, and they can smell self-interest from miles off. (We're media people ourselves, so we know whereof we speak.)

3. Follow HARO (@skydiver). HARO stands for Help A Reporter Out, and it's the brainchild of Peter Shankman, who regularly posts inquiries from reporters looking for sources.

twitter

TrackThis

Follow

Track Your
Packages over
Twitter Direct
Messages

1. Follow @TrackThis

2. Send a Direct
Message to TrackThis
like:
123456789123 New PC

3. Sit Back and Wait!
We'll send you a DM
when your package
moves

UseTrackThis.com

Created by @pb30

Over 100,000 package
been sent! Thanks to
has shared @TrackTh
followers!
8:25 AM Mar 29th from web

If you've followed @TrackThis, but aren
email mail@usetrackthis.com or try late
limits.
9:43 AM Mar 7th from web

We're a bit behind on updates due to a
catching up now.
12:24 PM Feb 25th from web

Some users have had issues receiving
into the issue. You may want to use ou

Integrate Twitter with your products

Twitter has an API (for you non-geeks, that's a data service), which means that if you have a web-based product or service, you may be able to integrate Twitter right into your site.

For example, personal finance site Wesabe lets you twitter your expenses directly to your account. TrackThis lets you use Twitter DMs to track your packages. iMeem, a social network for sharing cool media, lets you twitter out the music you're listening to.

Companies with integrations say their **users who avail themselves of the Twitter features are often their most avid fans.**

Of course, you can also build independent services right on top of the Twitter API. One of our favorites is **StockTwits** (http://stocktwits.com), which turns twittered ticker symbols into links that take you to real-time listings of all the posts about that company.

For more information about building your own Twitter applications and integrations, check out *Twitter API: Up and Running* by Kevin Makice (@kmakice) (O'Reilly Media, 2009; http://oreilly.com/catalog/9780596154615).

Name Paw Luxury
Web http://www.pawlux...
Bio eco-living for the everyday
dog - We offer eco-friendly,
organic, natural dog products
made in the USA. Contact:
Bark@PawLux.com

18,140   16,999   3,717
following   followers   updates

Name Web 2.0 Expo
Location SF, NY, online...
Web http://web2expo.com
Bio Web 2.0 Expo event &
community updates here.
Team blog -
http://blog.web2expo.com

12,467   11,335   1,297
following   followers   updates

Name rubbermaid
Location Huntersville, NC
Web http://blog.rubbe...
Bio All about Organization -
Currently tweeted by Jim
Deitzel

2,731   2,610   1,098
following   followers   updates

Name Graco
Location Exton, PA
Web http://blog.graco...
Bio Tweets from the Graco
team @lindsaylebresco (LL)
and Amy Trice (Customer
Service) (AT)

992   1,223   310
following   followers   updates

Follow everyone who follows you (almost)

Individuals have a lot of choice in whom and how many they follow, but businesses have less latitude. Because when somebody follows you, they're saying, "I'm interested in you and in having conversations with you." When you follow them back, **you're sending the same message, which will probably delight them.** In addition, following back opens the DM channel (described in Chapter 1), which can be key for customer support.

When you don't follow back, you can appear distant, disinterested or arrogant—exactly the opposite of what your organization is likely aiming for on Twitter.

That said, there are pitfalls to following all your followers. First, it takes time (though there are third-party programs that will auto-follow for you). Second, you can easily wind up following spammers, porn stars and other people you may not want associated with your company.

If you have time to check out each follower, great. If not, we recommend not sweating it too much and following back everyone, though you might skip the accounts with vulgar names.

By the way, if you find that following everyone means you can't keep on top of important accounts, use one of the tricks described in Chapter 5 to keep track of high-priority accounts.

Twist :: see trends in twitter

american idol, lost

Show trends

Tip: you can compare various topics, separate them with commas

Try these searches: morning,night work,party blackberry,iphone

Mentions chart

[What's this?]

Mentions of each topic during the past 7 days

Embed this chart in your site

Showing in this chart: **american idol** lost

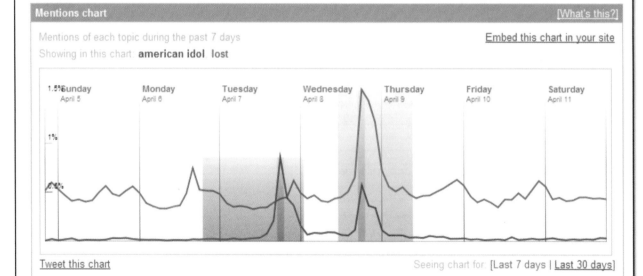

Tweet this chart

Seeing chart for: [Last 7 days | Last 30 days]

Three key tools for business accounts

As a business twitterer, you're likely to need a few **extra-strength tools for analyzing trends and managing your accounts.** Here are a handful we like a lot:

1. Twist (http://twist.flaptor.com) lets you compare the incidence of different topics on Twitter. It's great for getting a sense of whether one idea is more popular than others.

2. TweepDiff (http://tweepdiff.com) is a great tool for comparing the followers of your various accounts. It's handy when you're wondering whether there's a big overlap in the constituents for different accounts.

3. CoTweet (http://cotweet.com) is a third-party client designed for corporate use. It's got an array of thoughtful features to help you manage multiple posters and multiple accounts. The downside? As we were going to press, CoTweet was still in private beta—with a promise to release publicly in early summer. Keep an eye out.

Thanks for **helping and inspiring** us on this edition:
@abdelazer @abdur @adam @adamwitwer @biz @bgreelee
@bonniedone @chrisbrogan @christinew @dalepd @danmil
@deanmeistr @digitalroyalty @doctorow @dontgetcaught @ediefr
@ellnmllr @ericries @ev @fineyoungknife @fredwilson
@genny_spencer @gnat @grader @heymarci @hotdogsladies @jack
@jamesoreilly @jeffpulver @jenbee @jeremy @jimog @jkrums
@jokerwonga @joshmilstein @jowyang @jwikert @kanter
@karensatoreilly @kathysierra @kati @katmeyer @keppie_careers
@laurelatoreilly @lmilstein @maggie @mala @markfrauenfelder
@mashable @mattcutts @matthewburton @naypinya @oreillybrett
@padmasree @pahlkadot @petermeyers @pistachio @prnewswire
@sacca @saragoldstein @sarapeyton @sarawinge @sdmass
@skydiver @sreenet @terrie @the_real_shaq @tonystubblebine @veen
@venturehacks @wesabe @xenijardin @zappos @zoefinkel

Continuing the conversation

We want to have a conversation with you about new uses of Twitter and the future of this book. We'll be updating it regularly with what we learn from you. Post comments using the hashtag #TwitterBook, and also feel free to reach out to us: @timoreilly and @sarahm.

For great Twitter tips and resources, follow Sarah's additional account: @TweetReport.

INDEX

233

234